NATIONAL DIRECTORY
FOR THE FORMATION, MINISTRY,
AND LIFE OF PERMANENT DEACONS
IN THE UNITED STATES

NATIONAL DIRECTORY FOR THE FORMATION, MINISTRY, AND LIFE OF PERMANENT DEACONS IN THE UNITED STATES

Including the Secondary Documents
BASIC STANDARDS FOR READINESS
and
VISIT OF CONSULTATION TEAMS TO DIOCESAN PERMANENT DIACONATE FORMATION PROGAMS

This *National Directory for the Formation, Ministry, and Life of Permanent Deacons in the United States* is intended to serve the entire Catholic Church in the United States. Its principles, norms, and pastoral applications are directed specifically to the Latin Rite. Nonetheless, it may be of assistance as a consistent reference for all Churches *sui iuris* in the United States in the preparation of the adaptations necessary to address the particular traditions, pastoral life, and requirements of the *Code of Canons of the Eastern Churches.*

UNITED STATES CONFERENCE OF CATHOLIC BISHOPS

The document National Directory for the *Formation, Ministry, and Life of Permanent Deacons in the United States* was developed by the Bishops' Committee on the Diaconate of the United States Conference of Catholic Bishops (USCCB). It was approved by the full body of United States Catholic bishops at its June 2003 General Meeting, received the subsequent *recognitio* of the Holy See, and has been authorized for publication by the undersigned.

Msgr. William P. Fay
General Secretary, USCCB

Cover art: Scala/Art Resource, NY

First Printing, February 2005

ISBN 1-57455-368-2

Office of the President

3211 FOURTH STREET NE · WASHINGTON DC 20017-1194 · 202-541-3100 · FAX 202-541-3166

Most Reverend Wilton D. Gregory, S.L.D.
Bishop of Belleville

United States Conference of Catholic Bishops

DECREE OF PROMULGATION

In June 2003, the members of the United States Conference of Catholic Bishops approved the *National Directory for the Formation, Life and Ministry of Permanent Deacons in the United States*.

This action of the United States Conference of Catholic Bishops, made in accord with canon 236 of the *Code of Canon Law* and with n. 15 of *Ratio fundamentalis institutionis diaconorum permanentium*, was confirmed *ad quinquennium experimenti gratia* by the Congregations for Catholic Education and for Clergy (Prot. No. 78/2000), signed by Zenon Cardinal Grocholewski, prefect of the Congregation for Catholic Education, and Darío Cardinal Castrillón-Hoyos, prefect of the Congregation for Clergy, and dated October 30, 2004, to be observed in the formation of Permanent Deacons.

As President of the United States Conference of Catholic Bishops, I hereby declare that the effective date of this Decree of Promulgation will be December 26, 2004, the Feast of St. Stephen, Deacon and Martyr, with full implementation by August 10, 2005, the Feast of St. Lawrence of Rome, Deacon and Martyr.

Given at the offices of the United States Conference of Catholic Bishops in Washington, DC, November 15, 2004.

+ Wilton D. Gregory
Bishop of Belleville
President, USCCB

Monsignor William P. Fay
General Secretary, USCCB

TABLE OF CONTENTS

National Directory for the Formation, Ministry, and Life of Permanent Deacons in the United States

CHAPTER TWO

CHAPTER THREE

CHAPTER FOUR

CHAPTER FIVE

CHAPTER SIX

CHAPTER SEVEN

CHAPTER EIGHT

SECONDARY DOCUMENTS

FOREWORD

Throughout the last decade of the twentieth century, the Congregation for Catholic Education and the Congregation for the Clergy devoted considerable attention to the ordained ministries of priest and deacon. After the publication of the *Basic Norms for the Formation of Priests* and the *Directory on the Ministry and Life of Priests* in 1994, these two Congregations took up the same issues related to the ordained ministry of permanent deacons. In February 1998, they promulgated the *Basic Norms for the Formation of Permanent Deacons* and the *Directory on the Life and Ministry of Permanent Deacons*. In a Joint Declaration and Introduction, the prefects of these two Congregations offered these documents as directives "of which due account is to be taken by the Episcopal Conferences when preparing their respective 'Rationes.' As with the *Ratio fundamentalis institutionis sacerdotalis*, the Congregation offers this aid to the various Episcopates to facilitate them in discharging adequately the prescriptions of canon 236 of the Code of Canon Law and to ensure for the Church, unity, earnestness and completeness in the formation of permanent Deacons."[1]

After years of extensive consultation and preparation, the *National Directory for the Formation, Ministry, and Life of Permanent Deacons in the United States* received the *recognitio* from the Holy See on October 30, 2004. The *National Directory* was then officially promulgated by the president of the United States Conference of Catholic Bishops, on December 26, 2004, the Feast of St. Stephen, Deacon and Martyr.

On behalf of my predecessors who served as chairmen of the Bishops' Committee on the Diaconate in directing the preparation of this *National Directory*—Bishop Edward U. Kmiec, Bishop Gerald F. Kicanas, and Bishop Robert C. Morlino—and all the bishops who served on the committee during this period, I wish to acknowledge the extraordinary contribution made by the Rev. Msgr. Theodore W. Krauss of the Diocese of Oakland, California, who served as the project coordinator of the *National Directory* project. His most generous and skillful service in guiding the efforts of the many consultants, researchers, and other experts who contributed to the work of the committee is most gratefully appreciated.

Through much of the process, the work of the committee was greatly aided by two expert consultants: Rev. Kevin Irwin who served as theological consultant, and the Rev. Msgr. William A. Varvaro who served as canonical consultant. Providing overall wisdom and guidance were Cardinal Adam Maida and Bishop Donald W. Wuerl of Pittsburgh, who served as episcopal consultants to the committee.

I would like to offer a word about the organization of the documents presented in this volume. There are two major sections to this book. The first section contains the official *National Directory for the Formation, Ministry, and Life of Permanent Deacons in the United States*. This is the primary text, the text for which the *recognitio* has been received.

The second section consists of two secondary documents prepared as resources for the implementation of the *National Directory*. The first of these resource documents contains the *Basic Standards* for the formation of permanent deacons in the United States. Prepared by the Bishops' Committee on the Diaconate following considerable consultation in tandem with the *National Directory*, these *Standards* were approved by a vote of the full body of bishops in June 2000.

The second of these resource documents is the sixth revision of the committee document *Visit of Consultation Teams to Diocesan Permanent Diaconate Formation Programs*. This document is designed as an aid to the diocesan bishop and his staff in providing a mechanism for both program self-evaluation and for a formal visit and consultation by the Bishops' Committee on the Diaconate as outlined in the *National Directory*. This continues a resource offered by the Bishops' Committee on the Diaconate since the earliest days of the implementation of the permanent diaconate in the United States.

In the name of the Bishops' Committee on the Diaconate and the United States Conference of Catholic Bishops, I express our gratitude for the participation of all who assisted in the preparation of the *National Directory* and its related resources. Our heartfelt thanks to all those who serve so generously as deacons, as well as their families, pastors, and co-workers in ministry.

Bishop Frederick F. Campbell
Diocese of Columbus, Ohio
Chair, Bishops' Committee on the Diaconate

1 Congregation for Catholic Education and Congregation for the Clergy, "Joint Declaration and Introduction," *Basic Norms for the Formation of Permanent Deacons/Directory for the Ministry and Life of Permanent Deacons* (Vatican City: Libreria Editrice Vaticana, 1998), p. 8.

ABBREVIATIONS

ADUS Pope John Paul II, *The Heart of the Diaconate: Servants of the Mysteries of Christ and Servants of Your Brothers and Sisters*, Address to Deacons of the United States, Detroit, Michigan (September 19, 1987)

BNFPD Congregation for Catholic Education, *Basic Norms for the Formation of Permanent Deacons (Ratio Fundamentalis Institutionis Diaconorum Permanentium)* (Washington, DC: United States Catholic Conference, 1998)

CCC *Catechism of the Catholic Church*, 2nd ed. (Washington, DC : United States Conference of Catholic Bishops-Libreria Editrice Vaticana, 2000)

CIC Canon Law Society of America, trans., *Code of Canon Law Latin-English Edition (Codex Iuris Canonici)* (Washington, DC: Canon Law Society of America, 1983)

CL Congregation for Divine Worship and Discipline of the Sacraments, Circular Letter, *Scrutinies Regarding Suitability of Candidates for Orders*, Prot. No. 589/97 (November 28, 1997)

DMLPD Congregation for the Clergy, *Directory for the Ministry and Life of Permanent Deacons (Directorium Pro Ministerio et Vita Diaconorum Permanentium)* (Washington, DC: United States Catholic Conference, 1998)

FP Bishops' Committee on Marriage and Family, National Conference of Catholic Bishops, *A Family Perspective in Church and Society, Tenth Anniversary Edition* (Washington, DC: United States Catholic Conference, 1998)

GS Second Vatican Council, *Pastoral Constitution on the Church in the Modern World (Gaudium et Spes)* (Washington, DC: United States Catholic Conference, 1965)

LG   Second Vatican Council, *Dogmatic Constitution on the Church (Lumen Gentium)* (Washington, DC: United States Catholic Conference, 1964)

NSD (1996)   Bishops' Committee on the Permanent Diaconate, National Conference of Catholic Bishops, *A National Study on the Permanent Diaconate of the Catholic Church in the United States, 1994-1995* (Washington, DC: United States Catholic Conference, 1996)

OE   Second Vatican Council, *Decree on the Catholic Eastern Churches (Orientalium Ecclesiarum)*. In *Vatican Council II: Vol. 1: The Conciliar and Post Conciliar Documents*, Austin Flannery, ed. (Northport, NY: Costello, 1996).

PDG (1984)   Bishops' Committee on the Permanent Diaconate, National Conference of Catholic Bishops, *Permanent Deacons in the United States: Guidelines on Their Formation and Ministry, 1984 Revision* (Washington, D.C.: United States Catholic Conference, 1985)

PDO   Pope John Paul II, *The Permanent Deacon's Ordination*, Address to the Plenary Assembly of the Congregation for the Clergy (November 30, 1995)

PDV   Pope John Paul II, Post-Synodal Apostolic Exhortation, *I Will Give You Shepherds (Pastores Dabo Vobis)* (Washington, DC: United States Catholic Conference, 1992)

SC   Second Vatican Council, *Constitution on the Sacred Liturgy (Sacrosanctum Concilium)*. In *Vatican Council II: Vol. 1: The Conciliar and Post Conciliar Documents*, Austin Flannery, ed. (Northport, NY: Costello, 1996).

STVI   Bishops' Committee on the Liturgy and Bishops' Committee on the Permanent Diaconate, National Conference of Catholic Bishops, *The Deacon: Minister of Word and Sacrament, Study Text VI* (Washington, DC: United States Catholic Conference, 1979)

PRAYER TO THE BLESSED VIRGIN MARY

MARY

Teacher of faith, who by your obedience to the Word of God have cooperated in a remarkable way with the work of redemption, make the ministry of deacons effective by teaching them to hear the Word and to proclaim it faithfully.

MARY

Teacher of charity, who by your total openness to God's call have cooperated in bringing to birth all the Church's faithful, make the ministry and the life of deacons fruitful by teaching them to give themselves totally to the service of the People of God.

MARY

Teacher of prayer, who through your maternal intercession have supported and helped the Church from her beginnings, make deacons always attentive to the needs of the faithful by teaching them to come to know the value of prayer.

MARY

Teacher of humility, who by constantly knowing yourself to be the servant of the Lord were filled with the Holy Spirit, make deacons docile instruments in Christ's work of redemption by teaching them the greatness of being the least of all.

MARY

Teacher of that service which is hidden, who by your everyday and ordinary life filled with love knew how to cooperate with the salvific plan of God in an exemplary fashion, make deacons good and faithful servants by teaching them the joy of serving the Church with an ardent love.[1]

NOTE

1   Adapted from DMLPD, p. 141.

NATIONAL DIRECTORY
FOR THE FORMATION, MINISTRY, AND LIFE OF PERMANENT DEACONS IN THE UNITED STATES

PREFACE

I. The Diaconate in the Second Vatican Council and the Post-Conciliar Period: A Historical Overview[1]

1.   One of the great legacies of the Second Vatican Council was its renewal and encouragement of the order of deacons throughout the entire Catholic Church. The Council's decisions on the diaconate flowed out of the bishops' discussions on the sacramental nature of the Church. The Fathers of the Council present in concise, descriptive, and complementary images a comprehensive magisterial teaching: The Church is "mystery," "sacrament," "communion," and "mission."[2] The Church is "like a sacrament or as a sign and instrument both of a very closely knit union with God and of the unity of the whole human race. . . ."[3] "In her whole being and in all her members, the Church is sent to announce, bear witness, make present, and spread the mystery of the communion of the Holy Trinity."[4] This "missionary mandate"[5] is the Church's sacred right and obligation.[6] Through the proclamation of God's word, in sacramental celebrations, and in response to the needs of others, especially in her ministry of charity and justice, "the Church is Christ's instrument . . . 'the universal sacrament of salvation,' by which Christ is 'at once manifesting and actualizing the mystery of God's love for men.'"[7]

The diaconate: legacy of the Second Vatican Council

2.   Central to the Second Vatican Council's teaching on the Church is the service or ministry bestowed by Christ upon the apostles and their successors. The office of bishop "is a true service, which in sacred literature is significantly called a 'diakonia' or ministry."[8] The Council Fathers teach that the bishops, with priests and deacons as helpers, have by divine institution taken the place of the apostles as pastors of the Church.[9] Priests and deacons are seen as complementary but subordinate participants in the one apostolic ministry bestowed by Christ upon the apostles, with Peter as their head, and continued through their successors, the bishops, in union with the Roman Pontiff.[10] When discussing Holy Orders as one of the sacraments "at the service of communion" (along with Matrimony), the *Catechism of the Catholic Church* teaches that these two sacraments "are directed towards the salvation of others; if they

An apostolic ministry

contribute as well to personal salvation, it is through service to others that they do so. They confer a particular mission in the Church and serve to build up the People of God."[11]

3.   In the Dogmatic Constitution on the Church, the Decree on the Missionary Activity of the Church, and the Decree on the Catholic Eastern Churches, the Second Vatican Council reestablished the diaconate "as a proper and permanent rank of the hierarchy."[12] The Sacred Order of Deacons is to be "a driving force for the Church's service or diakonia toward the local Christian communities, and as a sign or sacrament of the Lord Christ himself, who 'came not to be served but to serve.'"[13] "The deacon's ministry of service is linked with the missionary dimension of the Church: the missionary efforts of the deacon will embrace the ministry of the word, the liturgy, and works of charity which, in their turn, are carried into daily life. Mission includes witness to Christ in a secular profession or occupation."[14] Further, "neither should the prospect of the mission ad gentes be lacking, wherever circumstances require and permit it."[15] In its renewal the Order of Deacons is permanently restored as "a living icon of Christ the Servant within the Church."[16]

4.   Following the closing of the Second Vatican Council, Pope Paul VI formally implemented the renewal of the diaconate. In his apostolic letter *Sacrum Diaconatus Ordinem*, he reestablished the Order of Deacons as a permanent ministry in the Catholic Church.[17] The apostolic constitution *Pontificalis Romani Recognito* promulgated new liturgical rites for the conferral of the Sacrament of Holy Orders upon bishops, priests, and deacons in the Latin Rite.[18] The apostolic letter *Ad Pascendum* established norms concerning the Order of Deacons.[19] The apostolic letter *Ministeria Quaedam* addressed the suppression in the Latin Rite of first tonsure, the minor orders, and the subdiaconate; established norms for entrance into the clerical state; and instituted the ministries of reader and acolyte.[20]

II. The Diaconate in the United States

5.   Since the Second Vatican Council consigned the decision of the restoration of the diaconate to individual episcopal conferences, the bishops of the United States voted in the spring of 1968 to peti-

tion the Holy See for authorization. In their letter of May 2, 1968, the bishops presented the following reasons for the request:

1. To complete the hierarchy of sacred orders and to enrich and strengthen the many and various diaconal ministries at work in the United States with the sacramental grace of the diaconate
2. To enlist a new group of devout and competent men in the active ministry of the Church
3. To aid in extending needed liturgical and charitable services to the faithful in both large urban and small rural communities
4. To provide an official and sacramental presence of the Church in areas of secular life, as well as in communities within large cities and sparsely settled regions where few or no priests are available
5. To provide an impetus and source for creative adaptations of diaconal ministries to the rapidly changing needs of our society

6.   On August 30, 1968, the Apostolic Delegate informed the United States bishops that Pope Paul VI had agreed to their request. In November of that year, a standing committee on the diaconate was created by the National Conference of Catholic Bishops (NCCB).21 In 1971, the conference approved and authorized the publication of the committee's document, *Permanent Deacons in the United States: Guidelines on Their Formation and Ministry*.[22] These *Guidelines* served the Church in the United States well as it began to assimilate the new ministry of deacons.[23] In February 1977, the committee organized a comprehensive study "to assess the extent to which the vision" for the diaconate had been realized.[24] The results of that appraisal were published in 1981 under the title *A National Study of the Permanent Diaconate in the United States*.[25] The report acknowledged that the purpose of the diaconate and its integration into the life of the Church in the United States had not yet been fully realized. Building on this *Study*, the NCCB commissioned the revision of the 1971 *Guidelines*. In November 1984, new guidelines were published with the release of *Permanent Deacons in the United States: Guidelines on Their Formation and Ministry, 1984 Revision*.[26]

USCCB Committee
on the Diaconate

A national catechesis

7.   The committee approved and authorized the publication of a series of monographs as part of a structured national catechesis on the diaconate. In collaboration with the committee, the Bishops' Committee on the Liturgy issued the document *The Deacon: Minister of Word and Sacrament, Study Text VI* (1979), which was devoted to the liturgical ministries of the deacon.[27] A second monograph addressed *The Service Ministry of the Deacon* (1988),[28] and a third monograph, *Foundations for the Renewal of the Diaconate* (1993), offered an international and historical perspective on the theology of the diaconate.[29] In 1998, the committee sponsored the production of a videotape, *Deacons: Ministers of Justice and Charity*, that highlighted some of the diverse service ministries of deacons in the United States.[30]

III. Recent Developments

8.   The documents of the Second Vatican Council convey "a great deal about bishops and laity and very little about priests and deacons."[31] In 1990, Pope John Paul II convened an Extraordinary Synod of Bishops to consider the life and ministry of priests within the Church in order "to close this gap on behalf of priests with the completion of some important initiatives . . . for example . . . the publication of the post-synodal Apostolic Exhortation *Pastores Dabo Vobis*[32] and, as an implementation of this document, the *Directory on the Ministry and Life of Priests.*[33]"[34]

Vatican Congregations' plenary assembly

9.   Seeking further to promote "a certain unity of direction and clarification of concepts, as well as . . . practical encouragement and more clearly defined pastoral objectives,"[35] the Congregation for the Clergy and the Congregation for Catholic Education organized a plenary assembly to study the diaconate. This gathering responded to concerns that had surfaced through the *ad limina* visits and reports of the bishops since the restoration of the diaconate was begun.[36] The members of the congregations and their consultants convened in November 1995. Pope John Paul II met with the participants and focused his comments on the identity, mission, and ministry of the deacon in the Church.[37]

10.   Following this plenary assembly, the Congregation for the Clergy published a *Directory for the Ministry and Life of Permanent Deacons* and concurrently, the Congregation for Catholic Education issued *Basic Norms for the Formation of Permanent Deacons*. Both documents provide episcopal conferences with directives and norms on the selection, formation, and pastoral care of aspirants, candidates, and deacons in accord with the intent of the Second Vatican Council and the subsequent teachings of Pope Paul VI and Pope John Paul II.[38] These documents were promulgated as a joint text by Pope John Paul II on February 22, 1998, the Feast of the Chair of Peter.[39]

Directory for the Ministry and Life of Permanent Deacons

Basic Norms for the Formation of Permanent Deacons

11.   In 1995-1996, the Bishops' Committee on the Diaconate, under the chairmanship of Most Rev. Dale J. Melczek, issued three documents: (1) *Protocol for the Incardination/Excardination of Deacons*, (2) *Policy Statement: Self-Study Instrument and Consultation Team Procedures*,[40] and (3) *A National Study on the Permanent Diaconate in the Catholic Church in the United States, 1994-1995*.[41] This *Study* focused on concerns that had surfaced at a special assembly of the Conference that was convened to address vocations and future church leadership. Those concerns included the identity of the deacon, his effective incorporation into the pastoral ministries of dioceses and parishes, and the need for better screening and training.[42] The *Study* confirmed the success of the restoration of the diaconate in the United States in terms of the number of vocations and in its significant, almost indispensable service to parochial communities. However, the *Study* also substantiates the concerns raised by the bishops and provides guidance in addressing them.[43]

Development of the diaconate in the United States

12.   In 1994, the committee organized a national conference for deacons. Its purpose was to celebrate the twenty-fifth anniversary of their restoration in the Church in the United States. The first National Catholic Diaconate Conference was convened in the Archdiocese of New Orleans. The theme of this conference was *Diaconate: A Great and Visible Sign of the Work of the Holy Spirit*. In June 1997, the participants gathered in the Archdiocese of Milwaukee and there explored the theme *The Deacon in a Diaconal Church: Minister of Justice and Charity*. A third conference was convened in June 2000 in the Diocese of Oakland; the theme of this Jubilee Year 2000 conference was *The Deacon in the Third Millennium—New Evangelization*.[44]

National Catholic Diaconate Conference

IV. The Development of This *National Directory*

13.   In March 1997, Most Rev. Edward U. Kmiec, chairman of the Bishops' Committee on the Diaconate,[45] convened two subcommittees to oversee the revision of the 1984 *Guidelines*. He named Most Rev. Howard J. Hubbard, D.D., and Most Rev. William E. Lori, S.T.D., members of the committee, as co-chairmen for the revision. He appointed Rev. Msgr. Theodore W. Kraus, Ph.D., past president of the National Association of Diaconate Directors, to serve as the project director. The members of both subcommittees brought varied professional and personal experience to the work and were representative of the geographic, cultural, and social profile of the Church in the United States.[46] Their work was assisted by Rev. Kevin Irwin, S.T.D., theological consultant to the committee; Rev. Msgr. William A. Varvaro, S.T.L., J.C.D., canonical consultant; and Deacon John Pistone, then-Executive Director of the Secretariat for the Diaconate, National Conference of Catholic Bishops. In November 1998, Most Rev. Gerald F. Kicanas., S.T.L., Ph.D., was elected by the conference as chairman of the committee. He invited Adam Cardinal Maida, J.C.L., J.D., S.T.L., and Most Rev. Donald W. Wuerl, S.T.D., to assist the committee as episcopal consultants in furthering the development of the document. Extensive consultation with the bishops and the major superiors of men religious, as well as diocesan directors of the diaconate and the executives of national diaconate organizations, preceded the approval of the document by the National Conference of Catholic Bishops at its general meeting in June 2000. In November 2001, Most Rev. Robert C. Morlino, S.T.D., was elected by the conference as chairman of the committee. Under his chairmanship, the committee revised the document in response to the observations received in March, 2002, from the Congregation for Catholic Education and the Congregation for the Clergy. The document was then approved by the United States Conference of Catholic Bishops at its general meeting in June 2003.

V. The Objective and Interpretation of This *National Directory*

National directives

14.   This *Directory* is prescribed for the use of the diocesan bishop, as well as those responsible for its implementation. The specifica-

tions published in this *Directory* are to be incorporated by each diocese of the conference when preparing or updating its respective diaconal formation program and in formulating policies for the ministry and life of their deacons.[47]

15.   This *Directory* is normative throughout the United States Conference of Catholic Bishops and its territorial sees. Reflecting more than thirty-five years of experience with the reestablished diaconate in the United States, this *Directory* will guide and harmonize the formation programs drawn up by each diocese of the conference that "at times vary greatly from one to another."[48]

This *Directory* is normative

16.   When a diaconal formation program is introduced or substantially modified, or a program previously "on hold" is reactivated, the diocesan bishop is encouraged to submit a proposal to the Bishops' Committee on the Diaconate for its evaluation. The specific elements to be included in the proposal and applied by the committee in its review are listed in Appendix I of this *Directory*.

17.   Finally, this document adopts as its own the concluding directive of the Congregation for Catholic Education: May the ordinaries, "to whom the present document is given, ensure that it becomes an object of attentive reflection in communion with their priests and communities. It will be an important point of reference for those Churches in which the permanent diaconate is a living and active reality; for the others, it will be an effective invitation to appreciate the value of that precious gift of the Spirit which is diaconal service."[49]

This is "an important point of reference"

VI. Acknowledgments

18.   Gratefully conscious of those who have served on the Bishops' Committee on the Diaconate, as well as its subcommittees, the United States Conference of Catholic Bishops acknowledges the direction of Most Rev. Edward U. Kmiec, under whose chairmanship the present effort was begun, and Most Rev. Gerald F. Kicanas, under whose chairmanship the *National Directory* was formulated, as well as Most Rev. Robert C. Morlino, under whose chairmanship it has been brought to conclusion.

NOTES

1   There is one Sacred Order of Deacons. Some deacons, who are in transition to ordination to the priesthood, usually exercise the Order of Deacons for a brief period of time. The vast majority of deacons live and exercise it, however, as a permanent rank of the hierarchy in both the Latin and Eastern Catholic Churches. This *Directory* addresses only the formation, ministry, and life of permanent deacons.

In 1995, as authorized by the General Secretary of the National Conference of Catholic Bishops, the word "permanent" was discontinued in the title of the bishops' committee, in the National Conference of Catholic Bishops' Secretariat for the Diaconate, and in its communiqués. In this text, therefore, the word "permanent" is not used unless it is contained in a specific quotation or in the title or committee of a publication. When the word "diaconate" is mentioned in this text, it refers to those who seek to be or are ordained permanent deacons.

In 2001, the National Conference of Catholic Bishops, the "canonical entity," and the United States Catholic Conference, the "the civil entity," were canonically and civilly reconstituted as the United States Conference of Catholic Bishops. This reconstituted entity is implied in this document except in those circumstances where the text requires reference to the previous nomenclatures.

2   Extraordinary Synod of Bishops, Final Report, *Ecclesia Sub Verbo Dei Mysteria Christi Celebrans Pro Salute Mundi* (December 7, 1995).

3   LG, no. 1.

4   CCC, no. 738.

5   Ibid., no. 849.

6   Second Vatican Council, *Decree on the Missionary Activity of the Church* (*Ad Gentes Divinitus*) (AGD) (December 7, 1965) (Washington, D.C.: United States Catholic Conference, 1965), nos. 15-16.

7   CCC, no. 776. Cf. LG, nos. 9-17, 48; GS, nos. 1-3, 26-30, 32, 45.

8   LG, no. 24. Cf. Acts 1:17, 25; 21:19; Rom 11:13; 1 Tm 1:12; Pope John Paul II, Post-Synodal Apostolic Exhortation, *The Vocation and the Mission of the Lay Faithful in the Church and in the World* (*Christifideles Laici*) (December 30, 1988) (Washington, D.C.: United States Catholic Conference, 1988), no. 22.

9   Ibid., nos. 18, 20.

10   Ibid., nos. 20; cf. nos. 22-23.

11   CCC, no. 1534.

12   LG, no. 29. Cf. AGD, op. cit., nos. 15-16; OE, no. 17.

13   Pope Paul VI, Apostolic Letter, *Ad Pascendum* (AP) (August 15, 1972), citing Mt 20:28.

14   DMLPD, no. 27.

15   BNFPD, no. 88.

16   Ibid., no. 11.

17   Pope Paul VI, Apostolic Letter, *Sacrum Diaconatus Ordinem* (June 18, 1967).

18   Pope Paul VI, Apostolic Constitution, *Pontificalis Romani Recognito* (June 18, 1968).

19   AP, op. cit.

20   Pope Paul VI, Apostolic Letter, *Ministeria Quaedem* (August 15, 1972).

21   The committee's responsibilities, as authorized by the United States Conference of Catholic Bishops, are specified in Appendix II of this *Directory*.

22   Bishops' Committee on the Permanent Diaconate, National Conference of Catholic Bishops, *Permanent Deacons in the United States: Guidelines on Their Formation and Ministry* (Washington, D.C.: United States Catholic Conference, 1971). The committee, under its first chairman, Most Rev. Ernest L. Unterkoefler, prepared these *Guidelines*.

23   The diaconate has grown remarkably in the United States. According to statistics of the USCCB Secretariat for the Diaconate, there were, in 1971, 58 deacons and 529 candidates, and in 1975, 1,074 deacons and 2,243 candidates. By 1980, the number of deacons had quadrupled to 4,656, with 2,514 candidates. As of December 31, 2001, more than 14,000 deacons were serving in the dioceses of the United States and territorial sees. Only six dioceses had no incardinated deacons.

24   Bishops' Committee on the Permanent Diaconate, National Conference of Catholic Bishops, *A National Study of the Permanent Diaconate in the United States* (Washington, D.C.: United States Catholic Conference, 1981), p. 1.

25   Ibid.

26   PDG (1984). The committee under the chairmanship of Most Rev. John J. Snyder began the revision. It was completed under the chairmanship of Most Rev. John F. Kinney.

27   STVI.

28   Bishops' Committee on the Permanent Diaconate, National Conference of Catholic Bishops, *Service Ministry of the Deacon*, Rev. Timothy J. Shugrue, author, (Washington, D.C.: United States Catholic Conference, 1988).

28   Bishops' Committee on the Permanent Diaconate, National Conference of Catholic Bishops, *Foundations for the Renewal of the Diaconate* (Washington, D.C.: United States Catholic Conference, 1993).

30   Bishops' Committee on the Diaconate, National Conference of Catholic Bishops, *Deacons: Ministers of Justice and Charity* [video], Deacon Richard Folger, editor, (1998).

31   Most Rev. Crescenzio Sepe, Secretary of the Congregation for the Clergy, Address to the National Catholic Diaconate Conference, New Orleans, La. (July 21, 1994).

32   PDV.

33   Congregation for the Clergy, *Directory on the Ministry and Life of Priests* (Washington, D.C.: Libreria Editrice Vaticana-United States Catholic Conference, 1994).

34   Most Rev. Crescenzio Sepe, op. cit.

35   BNFPD and DMLPD, Joint Declaration.

36   These concerns centered upon an incorrect understanding of the role of the deacon in the hierarchical structure of the Church, of the doctrine on ministries, on the role of the laity and the role of women, as well as concerns regarding selection, adequate intellectual formation, and proper pastoral ministries for deacons. Cf. Most Rev. Crescenzio Sepe, op. cit.

37   PDO.

38   BNFPD and DMLPD, Introduction, no. 2; cf. BNFPD, no. 14.

39   BNFPD, no. 90; DMLPD, no. 82. Additional Vatican documents relevant to the formation and ministry of deacons include the following: (1) *Guide for Catechists* (1993), promulgated by the Congregation for Evangelization of Peoples, which proposes educational and formational models. As required by the Congregation for Catholic Education in BNFPD, diaconal formation is to encompass more than catechist formation and is to be more analogous to the formation of priests. *Guide for Catechists* provides universal norms for catechist formation. (2) The *General Directory for Catechesis* (1997), from the Congregation for the Clergy, provides insightful criteria in proposing appropriate adult education methodologies and for establishing perimeters for an authentic and complete theological study. The *Instruction on Certain Questions Regarding the Collaboration of the Non-Ordained Faithful in the Sacred Ministry of Priests* (1997), signed by the heads of eight dicasteries of the Holy See, establishes norms for appropriate collaboration between the ordained ministers of the Church and the non-ordained faithful. (3) In 1997, the Congregation for Divine Worship and the Discipline of the Sacraments issued a Circular Letter to diocesan bishops and religious ordinaries establishing criteria on the suitability of candidates to be admitted to sacred orders and further directing the establishment of a diocesan board to oversee the scrutinies of candidates before the reception of the rite of candidacy, the ministry of lector, the ministry of acolyte, and ordination to the diaconate and priesthood. [The text abbreviation in this document is CL.] This document is essential in the formulation of admission and selection policies for diaconal candidates. (4) The Pontifical Council for Promoting Christian Unity issued a supplementary document to its *Directory for the Application of Principles and Norms on Ecumenism* (1993), namely, *The Ecumenical Dimension in the Formation of Those Engaged in Pastoral Work* (1997). This document specifies that an ecumenical dimension is to be included in diaconal formation and ministry. (5) The encyclical letter *On the Relationship Between Faith and Reason* (1998), promulgated by Pope John Paul II, establishes academic parameters to be included in the intellectual and human dimensions of diaconal formation. (6) The post-synodal apostolic exhortation *The Church in America* (1999), promulgated by Pope John Paul II, addresses the new evangelization in the Church in America and makes reference to the role of the deacon in that ministry.

40   Bishops' Committee on the Diaconate, National Conference of Catholic Bishops, Protocol for the Incardination/Excardination of Deacons (1995) and Policy Statement: Self-Study Instrument and Consultation Team Procedures (1995).

41   NSD (1996).

42   Joseph Cardinal Bernardin, "Summary Comments on the Permanent Diaconate," Special

Assembly of the National Conference of Catholic Bishops, St. John's Abbey, Collegeville, Minn. (June 9-16, 1986), in *Vocations and Future Church Leadership* (Washington, D.C.: United States Catholic Conference, 1986).

43   NSD (1996), pp. 13-16.

44   In 1994, Most Rev. Crescenzio Sepe, D.D., Secretary of the Congregation for the Clergy, addressed the National Catholic Diaconate Conference on the background and preparations being made for the plenary assembly scheduled for November 1995. In 1997, Cardinal Darío Castrillón Hoyos, Pro-Prefect of the Congregation for the Clergy, spoke on "The Deacon in the Life and Mission of the Church," providing insight on the *Directory* being prepared by the Congregation. In 2000, Most Rev. Gabriel Montalvo, Apostolic Nuncio to the United States, addressed the role of the deacon in the Church's mission of new evangelization.

45   See Note 1 above regarding the removal of the word "permanent" from title of the Bishops' Committee on the Diaconate.

46   The members of the Subcommittee on Formation and Curriculum included the following: Most Rev. Howard Hubbard, Bishop of Albany, N.Y. (chairman); [Deacon Ministry and Life] Deacon James Swiler, Director of Diaconate Formation, Archdiocese of New Orleans, La. (facilitator); Mrs. Bonnie Swiler, Archdiocese of New Orleans, La.; Sr. Yvonne Lerner, OSB, Director of Diaconate Formation, Diocese of Little Rock, Ark.; [Formation] Dr. Ann Healey, Director of Deacon Formation, Fort Worth, Texas (facilitator); Rev. Michael Galvan, Pastor, St. Joseph Church, Pinole, Calif.; Deacon James Keeley, Director of Diaconate Formation, Diocese of San Diego, Calif.; Mrs. Jeanne Schrempf, Director of Religious Education, Diocese of Albany, N.Y.; Deacon Enrique Alonso, President, National Association of Hispanic Deacons; [Diocesan Structures and Selection] Mr. Timothy C. Charek, Director, Deacon Formation Program, Archdiocese of Milwaukee, Wis. (facilitator); Most Rev. Dominic Carmon, SVD, Auxiliary Bishop of the Archdiocese of New Orleans, La., member of the Bishops' Committee on the Diaconate; Rev. Richard W. Woy, Vicar for Clergy, Archdiocese of Baltimore, Md.; [Curriculum] Deacon Stephen Graff, Dean of Students, St. Bernard's Institute, Rochester, N.Y. (facilitator); Rev. Msgr. Ernest J. Fiedler, Rector, Cathedral of the Immaculate Conception, Diocese of Kansas City, Mo., and former Executive Director, NCCB Secretariat for the Diaconate; Rev. Bryan Massingale, Vice Rector, St. Francis Seminary, Milwaukee, Wis.; Rev. Alejandro Castillo, SVD, Director of the Office for Hispanic Affairs, California Catholic Conference, Sacramento, Calif.; Rev. Robert Egan, SJ, St. Michael's Institute, Spokane, Wash.; Mr. Neal Parent, Executive Director, National Conference of Catechetical Leadership, Washington, D.C.; Dr. Seung Ai Yang, Professor of Scripture, The Jesuit School of Theology, Berkeley, Calif. The members of the Subcommittee for Theological and Canonical Revision included Most Rev. William Lori, Auxiliary Bishop of Washington, D.C. (chairman); [Theology] Rev. Msgr. Paul Langsfeld, Vice Rector, St. Mary's Seminary, Emmitsburg, Md. (facilitator); Deacon Samuel M. Taub, Diocese of Arlington, Va., former Executive Director, NCCB Secretariat for the Diaconate; Sr. Patricia Simpson, OP, Prioress, Dominican Sisters of San

Rafael, Calif., and former Director of Diaconate Formation, Diocese of Sacramento, Calif.; Rev. Frank Silva, Pastor, Immaculate Conception Church, Malden, Mass., and former Director of Diaconate, Archdiocese of Boston, Mass.; [Spirituality] Deacon William T. Ditewig, Director of Pastoral Services and Ministry Formation, Diocese of Davenport, Iowa (facilitator); Mrs. Diann Ditewig, Davenport, Iowa; Most Rev. Allen H. Vigneron, Auxiliary Bishop of the Archdiocese of Detroit, Mich., and Rector, Sacred Heart Major Seminary, Detroit, Mich.; Deacon James Condill, President, National Association of Deacon Organizations; [Ministry] Rev. Msgr. Timothy Shugrue, Pastor, Immaculate Conception Church, Montclair, N.J., and former Director of Diaconate, Archdiocese of Newark, N.J. (facilitator); Rev. Edward Salmon, Vicar, Diaconate Community, Archdiocese of Chicago, Ill.; Rev. Msgr. Joseph Roth, President, National Association of Diaconate Directors; Deacon John Stewart, President, National Association of African-American Catholic Deacons. Rev. Msgr. Theodore W. Kraus, Director of Diaconate, Diocese of Oakland, the *Directory's* project director, served *ex officio* on each subcommittee and working unit.

47   BNFPD and DMLPD, Joint Declaration; cf. BNFPD, nos. 14, 17.
48   BNFPD, nos. 2, 14.
49   BNFPD, no. 90.

CHAPTER ONE
DOCTRINAL UNDERSTANDING OF THE DIACONATE

I. Introduction

19. This *Directory* offers some theological points of reference based upon relevant magisterial teaching. As the Congregation for Catholic Education explains, "The almost total disappearance of the permanent diaconate from the Church of the West for more than a millennium has certainly made it more difficult to understand the profound reality of this ministry. However, it cannot be said for that reason that the theology of the diaconate has no authoritative points of reference. . . [T]hey are very clear, even if they need to be developed and deepened."[1]

Theological points of reference

II. The Sacramental Nature of the Church

20. The Second Vatican Council spoke of the Church as "mystery," "sacrament," "communion," and "mission":[2] "The Church is in Christ like a sacrament or as a sign and instrument both of a very closely knit union with God and of the unity of the whole human race."[3] The Church is the People of God, the Body of Christ, and the Temple of the Holy Spirit.[4] It is "the community of faith, hope and charity" as well as "an entity with visible delineation."[5] "But, the society [formed] with hierarchical [structures] and the Mystical Body of Christ . . .[is] not to be considered as two realities, nor are the visible assembly and the spiritual community, nor the earthly Church and the Church enriched with heavenly things; rather they form one complex reality, which coalesces from a divine and a human element."[6]

Church: One complex reality

21. Jesus Christ, through his ministry, life, death, and resurrection, established in human society and history a new and distinct reality, a community of men and women, through whom "He communicated truth and grace to all."[7] Through the Church, the Good News of Jesus Christ continues to be told and applied to the changing circumstances and challenges of human life. As Christians live their

Church as communion and mission

lives in the power of the Holy Spirit and in the assurance of Christ's return in glory, they offer to others a hope to live by, encouraging them also to embrace Christ and overcome the forces of evil. In the sacraments, which symbolize and make real again the gifts of God that are the origin, center, and goal of the Church's life, the power of Jesus Christ's redemption is again and again at work in the world. In her ministry of charity and justice, the Church "encompasses with love all who are afflicted with human suffering and in the poor and afflicted sees the image of her poor and suffering founder. She does all in her power to relieve their need and in them she strives to serve Christ "[8] Thus, in the communion of life, love, and service realized under the leadership of the successors of the apostles, a vision of reconciled humanity is offered to the world.

III. Ecclesial Communion and Mission

The Sacraments of Christian Initiation: Baptism, Confirmation, and Eucharist

Initiation into the
Church's communion
and mission

22.   Initiation into the Church, the Body of Christ, comes about first through the Sacrament of Baptism—the outpouring of the Holy Spirit. In Baptism, every member of the Church receives new life in the Spirit and becomes a member of Christ's Body—a participant in the new creation. This new life is strengthened in the Sacrament of Confirmation, through which the baptized receives the Spirit and is more perfectly bound to the Church and obliged to bear witness to Christ, to spread and defend the faith by word and deed. In the Sacrament of the Eucharist, the child of God receives the food of new life, the body and blood of Christ. In this Holy Communion, Christ unites each of the baptized to all the faithful in one body—the Church:

> Baptism, Confirmation, and Eucharist are sacraments of Christian initiation. They ground the common vocation of all Christ's disciples, a vocation to holiness and to the mission of evangelizing the world. They confer the graces needed for the life according to the Spirit during this life as pilgrims on the march towards the homeland.[9]

> Communion and mission are profoundly connected with each other, they interpenetrate and mutually imply each other, to the

point that communion represents both the source and the fruit of mission: communion gives rise to mission and mission is accomplished in communion. It is always the one and the same Spirit who calls together and unifies the Church and sends her to preach the Gospel "to the ends of the earth."[10]

The Sacrament of Holy Orders

23.   The Church, itself the great sacrament of Christ's presence, rejoices in another "outpouring of the Spirit"[11]—the Sacrament of Holy Orders. Out of the body of initiated believers—anointed in the Holy Spirit through the Sacrament of Baptism, strengthened in the Sacrament of Confirmation, and nurtured with the Bread of Life— Christ calls some to ordained service. The Church, discerning their vocational charism, asks the bishop to ordain them to *diakonia*.

Some are called to ordained service

24.   "Holy Orders is the sacrament through which the mission entrusted by Christ to his apostles [and their successors] continues to be exercised in the Church until the end of time."[12] Thus, it is the sacrament of apostolic ministry: "The mission of the Apostles, which the Lord Jesus continues to entrust to the Pastors of his people, is a true service, significantly referred to in Sacred Scripture as '*diakonia*,' namely, service or ministry."[13] This *diakonia* "is exercised on different levels by those who from antiquity have been called bishops, priests and deacons."[14] "The ordained ministries, apart from the persons who receive them, are a grace for the entire Church."[15]

Holy Orders: The sacrament of apostolic ministry

25.   The *Catechism of the Catholic Church* speaks of the Sacrament of Holy Orders in this way:

Catechism of the Catholic Church: Sacrament of Holy Orders

Catholic doctrine, expressed in the liturgy, the Magisterium, and the constant practice of the Church, recognizes that there are two degrees of ministerial participation in the priesthood of Christ: the episcopacy and the presbyterate. The diaconate is intended to help and serve them. For this reason the term *sacerdos* in current usage denotes bishops and priests but not deacons. Yet Catholic doctrine teaches that the degrees of priestly participation (episcopate and presbyterate) and the degree of service (diaconate) are all three conferred by a sacramental act called "ordination," that is, by the Sacrament of Holy Orders.[16]

The primacy of apostolic ministry

26.   St. Paul points out that the Holy Spirit is the source of all ministries in the Church and that these services are quite distinct.[17] The distribution of ministerial gifts follows a design set by Christ:

> In the building up of Christ's Body various members and functions have their part to play. There is only one Spirit who, according to His own richness and the needs of the ministries, gives His different gifts for the welfare of the Church. What has a special place among these gifts is the grace of the apostles to whose authority the Spirit Himself subjected even those who are endowed with charisms.[18]

IV. The Reestablished Order of Deacons

Diaconate: A permanent rank in the hierarchy

27.   The Fathers of the Second Vatican Council, taking seriously the role of the deacon to which St. Paul refers in his first letter to Timothy, remind us that "those who serve well as deacons gain good standing and much confidence in their faith in Christ Jesus."[19] It was for serious pastoral and theological reasons that the Council decided to reestablish the Order of Deacons as a permanent rank in the hierarchy of the Church.

The deacon: Configured to Christ the deacon

28.   The Sacrament of Holy Orders marks deacons "with an *imprint* ('character') which cannot be removed and which configures them to Christ, who made himself the 'deacon' or servant of all."[20] For this level of Holy Orders, Christ calls and the Church asks the bishop to ordain deacons to be consecrated witnesses to service. In his post-synodal exhortation *The Church in America*, Pope John Paul II makes his own the words of the bishops of that gathering: "We see with joy how deacons 'sustained by the grace of the Sacrament, in the ministry (*diakonia*) of the liturgy, of the word and of charity are at the service of the People of God, in communion with the Bishop and his priests.'"[21]

Deacon: Neither a lay person nor a priest, but a cleric

29.   Ordination confers an outpouring of the Holy Spirit. It configures the deacon to Christ's consecration and mission. It constitutes the deacon as "a sacred minister and a member of the hierarchy,"[22] with a distinct identity and integrity in the Church that marks him as neither a lay person nor a priest; rather, the deacon is a cleric who is ordained to *diakonia*, namely, a service to God's

People in communion with the bishop and his body of priests. "The principal function of the deacon, therefore, is to collaborate with the bishop and the priests in the exercise of a ministry which is not of their own wisdom but of the Word of God, calling all to conversion and holiness."[23]

30.   Referring to the traditional description of the deacon's *diakonia* to the Church and the bishop, Pope John Paul II observes that in an ancient text, the deacon's ministry is defined as a "service to the bishop."[24] This observation highlights the constant understanding of the Church that the deacon enjoys a unique relationship with his bishop. The Pope clearly has in view, therefore, the reason for not only the diaconate but the whole apostolic ministry: serving the discipleship of God's people. Pope John Paul II notes that

Service to the People of God

> the deacon's tasks include that of "promoting and sustaining the apostolic activities of the laity." To the extent he is more present and more involved than the priest in secular environments and structures, he should feel encouraged to foster closeness between the ordained ministry and lay activities, in common service to the kingdom of God.[25]

In particular, "a deeply felt need in the decision to reestablish the permanent diaconate," the Pope recalls, "was and is that of a greater and more direct presence of Church ministers in the various spheres of the family, work, school, etc., in addition to existing pastoral structures."[26] Deacons, both married and celibate, serve God's People by their witness to the gospel value of sacrificial love, a quality of life too easily dismissed in today's society. In their secular employment, deacons also make evident the dignity of human work. Contemporary society is in need of a "new evangelization which demands a greater and more generous effort on the part of [all] ordained ministers."[27] This is especially an opportunity and obligation for deacons in their secular professions to boldly proclaim and witness to the Gospel of life.

V. The Church's Ministry of the Word:
The Deacon as Evangelizer and Teacher

Herald of the Gospel

31.   The deacon participates as an evangelizer and teacher in the Church's mission of heralding the word. In the liturgy of the word, especially in the Eucharist or in those liturgies where he is the presiding minister, the deacon proclaims the Gospel. He may preach by virtue of ordination and in accord with the requirements of Canon Law.[28] Other forms of the deacon's participation in the Church's ministry of the word include catechetical instruction; religious formation of candidates and families preparing for the reception of the sacraments; leadership roles in retreats, evangelization, and renewal programs; outreach to alienated Catholics; and counseling and spiritual direction, to the extent that he is properly trained.[29] The deacon also strives to "transmit the word in [his] professional [life] either explicitly or merely by [his] active presence in places where public opinion is formed and ethical norms are applied."[30]

Witnessing the Word in his own life, the deacon leads people to their practice of charity and justice

32.   In these and many other formal and informal ways, the deacon leads the community to reflect on their communion and mission in Jesus Christ, especially impelling the community of believers to live lives of service. Because the deacon sacramentalizes service, he should proclaim the word in such a way that he first witnesses its empowerment in his own life. Then he can effectively challenge others to practice the Church's ministry of charity and justice in the social environments in which people live their baptismal vocation. By his own faithful practice of the spiritual and corporal works of mercy, the deacon "by word and example . . . should work so that all the faithful, in imitation of Christ, may place themselves at the constant service of their brothers and sisters."[31]

VI. The Church's Ministry of Liturgy:
The Deacon as Sanctifier

Liturgical ministry

33.   For the deacon, as for all members of the Church, the liturgy is "the summit toward which the activity of the Church is directed; at the same time it is the fount from which all the Church's power flows."[32] For the Church gathered at worship, moreover, the ministry of the deacon is a visible, grace-filled sign of the integral connection between sharing at the Lord's Eucharistic table and serving the

many hungers felt so keenly by all God's children. In the deacon's liturgical ministry, as in a mirror, the Church sees a reflection of her own diaconal character and is reminded of her mission to serve as Jesus did.

34.　In the context of the Church's public worship, because of its centrality in the life of the believing community, the ministry of the deacon in the threefold diakonia of the word, of the liturgy, and of charity is uniquely concentrated and integrated. "The diaconate is conferred through a special outpouring of the Spirit (*ordination*), which brings about in the one who receives it a specific conformation to Christ, Lord and servant of all."[33] "Strengthened by sacramental grace, they are dedicated to the people of God, in conjunction with the bishop and his body of priests, in a service of the liturgy of the word and of charity."[34]

An integral diakonia

35.　During the celebration of the Eucharistic liturgy, the deacon participates in specific penitential rites as designated in the *Roman Missal*. He properly proclaims the Gospel. He may preach the homily in accord with the provisions of Canon Law. He voices the needs of the people in the General Intercessions, needs with which he should have a particular and personal familiarity from the circumstances of his ministry of charity. The deacon assists the presider and other ministers in accepting the offerings of the people—symbolic of his traditional role in receiving and distributing the resources of the community among those in need—and he helps to prepare the gifts for sacrifice. During the celebration he helps the faithful participate more fully, consciously, and actively in the Eucharistic sacrifice,[35] may extend the invitation of peace, and serves as an ordinary minister of Communion. Deacons have a special responsibility for the distribution of the cup. Finally, he dismisses the community at the end of the eucharistic liturgy. Other liturgical roles for which the deacon is authorized include those of solemnly baptizing, witnessing marriages, bringing *viaticum* to the dying, and presiding over funerals and burials. The deacon can preside at the liturgies of the word and communion services in the absence of a priest. He may officiate at celebrations of the Liturgy of the Hours and at exposition and benediction of the Blessed Sacrament. He can conduct public rites of blessing, offer prayer services for the sick and dying, and administer the Church's sacramentals, as designated in the *Book of*

Liturgical functions

Blessings.[36] In the Eastern Catholic Churches, the liturgical ministries of deacons are prescribed by the legislative authority of each particular Church.

VII. The Church's Ministry of Charity and Justice: The Deacon as Witness and Guide

Service: The hallmark of faithfulness

36.   The deacon's ministry, as Pope John Paul II has said, "is the Church's service sacramentalized."[37] Therefore, the deacon's service in the Church's ministry of word and liturgy would be severely deficient if his exemplary witness and assistance in the Church's ministry of charity and justice did not accompany it. Thus, Pope John Paul II affirms both: "This is at the very heart of the diaconate to which you have been called: to be a servant of the mysteries of Christ and, at one and the same time, to be a servant of your brothers and sisters. That these two dimensions are inseparably joined together in one reality shows the important nature of the ministry which is yours by ordination."[38]

Service: The hallmark of faithfulness

37.   The deacon's service in the Church's ministry of charity and justice is integral to his service in the Church's ministry of word and liturgy. "The three contexts of the diaconal ministry . . . represent a unity in service at the level of divine Revelation: the ministry of the word leads to ministry at the altar, which in turn prompts the transformation of life by the liturgy, resulting in charity."[39] "As a [participant] in the one ecclesiastical ministry, [the deacon] is a specific sacramental sign, in the Church, of Christ the Servant. His role is to 'express the needs and desires of the Christian communities' and to be 'a driving force for service, or *diakonia*,' which is an essential part of the mission of the Church."[40] The ancient tradition appears to indicate that because the deacon was the servant at the table of the poor, he had his distinctive liturgical roles at the Table of the Lord. Similarly, there is a reciprocal correspondence between his role as a herald of the Gospel and his role as an articulator of the needs of the Church in the General Intercessions. In his formal liturgical roles, the deacon brings the poor to the Church and the Church to the poor. Likewise, he articulates the Church's concern for justice by being a driving force in addressing the injustices among God's people. He thus symbolizes in his roles the grounding of the Church's life in the Eucharist and the mission of the Church in her

loving service of the needy. In the deacon, in a unique way, is represented the integral relationship between the worship of God in the liturgy that recalls Jesus Christ's redemptive sacrifice sacramentally and the worship of God in everyday life where Jesus Christ is encountered in the needy. The deacon's service begins at the altar and returns there. The sacrificial love of Christ celebrated in the Eucharist nourishes him and motivates him to lay down his life on behalf of God's People.

38.   The apostles' decision to appoint ministers to attend to the needs of the Greek-speaking widows of the early Church at Jerusalem[41] has long been interpreted as a normative step in the evolution of ministry. It is seen as a practical response to Jesus' command during the Last Supper of mutual service among his followers. In washing his disciples' feet, Jesus as head and shepherd of the community modeled the service that he desired to be the hallmark of their faithfulness. This gave the disciples a powerful sign of the love of God that was, in Jesus himself, incarnate and intended to be forever enfleshed in the attitudes and behaviors of his followers.[42] The deacon, consecrated and conformed to the mission of Christ, Lord and Servant, has a particular concern for the vitality and genuineness of the exercise of *diakonia* in the life of the believing community. In a world hungry and thirsty for convincing signs of the compassion and liberating love of God, the deacon sacramentalizes the mission of the Church in his words and deeds, responding to the master's command of service and providing real-life examples of how to carry it out.

The washing of feet: The foundational model of diaconal service

VIII. An Intrinsic Unity

39.   By ordination, the deacon, who sacramentalizes the Church's service, is to exercise the Church's *diakonia*. Therefore, "the diaconal ministries, distinguished above, are not to be separated; the deacon is ordained for them all, and no one should be ordained who is not prepared to undertake each in some way."[43] "However, even if this inherent ministerial service is one and the same in every case, nevertheless, the concrete ways of carrying it out are diverse; these must be suggested, in each case, by the different pastoral situations of the single churches."[44] A deacon may also have greater abilities in one aspect of ministry; and, therefore, his service may be marked by one of them more than by the others. Fundamentally, however,

An intrinsic unity among the deacon's service ministries

there is an intrinsic unity in a deacon's ministry. In preaching the word, he is involved in every kind of missionary outreach. In sanctifying God's People through the liturgy, he infuses and elevates people with new meaning and with a Christian worldview. In bringing Christ's reign into every stratum of society, the deacon develops a Christian conscience among all people of good will, motivating their service and commitment to the sanctity of human life.

IX. Concluding Reflection

40.   When one reflects upon the Order of Deacons, it is worthwhile to recall the words from the ordination ritual of deacons:

> Like those once chosen by the Apostles for the ministry of charity, you should be men of good reputation, filled with wisdom and the Holy Spirit. Firmly rooted and grounded in faith, you are to show yourselves chaste and beyond reproach before God and man, as is proper for the ministers of Christ and the stewards of God's mysteries. Never allow yourselves to be turned away from the hope offered by the Gospel. Now you are not only hearers of this Gospel but also its ministers. Holding the mystery of faith with a clear conscience, express by your actions the Word of God which your lips proclaim, so that the Christian people, brought to life by the Spirit, may be a pure offering accepted by God. Then on the last day, when you go out to meet the Lord you will be able to hear him say, "Well done, good and faithful servant, enter into the joy of your Lord."[45]

NOTES

1   BNFPD, no. 3.

2   Extraordinary Synod of Bishops, Final Report, *Ecclesia Sub Verbo Dei Mysteria Christi Celebrans Pro Salute Mundi* (December 7, 1995).

3   LG, no. 1.

4   Ibid., no. 17.

5   Ibid., no. 8.

6   Ibid.

7   Ibid.

8   Ibid.

9   CCC, no. 1533.

10 Pope John Paul II, post-synodal Apostolic Exhortation, *The Vocation and the Mission of the Lay Faithful in the Church and in the World* (*Christifideles Laici*) (December 30, 1988) (Washington, D.C.: United States Catholic Conference, 1988), no. 32, citing Acts 1:8.

11 BNFPD, no. 5.

12 CCC, no. 1536.

13 Ibid., no. 22; cf. LG, no. 24.

14 LG, no. 28.

15 Pope John Paul II, *Christifideles Laici*, op. cit., no. 22.

16 CCC, no. 1554.

17 Cf. 1 Cor 12:4-11; Rom 12:4-8.

18 LG, no. 7.

19 1 Tm 3:13.

20 CCC, no. 1570.

21 Pope John Paul II, post-synodal Apostolic Exhortation, *The Church in America* (*Ecclesia in America*) (January 22, 1999) (Washington, D.C.: United States Catholic Conference, 1999), no. 42, citing LG, no. 29.

22 DMLPD, no. 1.

23 DMLPD, no. 23.

24 Pope John Paul II, General Audience, *Deacons Have Many Pastoral Functions* (October 13, 1993), no. 1, citing Hippolytus, *Apostolic Tradition*.

25 Ibid., no. 5, citing Pope Paul VI, Apostolic Letter, *Sacrum Diaconatus Ordinem*, (June 18, 1967), no. 22.

26 Pope John Paul II, General Audience, *Deacons Serve the Kingdom of God* (October 5, 1993), no. 6.

27 DMLPD, no. 26.

28 CIC, c. 764: "With due regard for the prescription of can. 765, presbyters and deacons possess the faculty to preach everywhere, to be exercised with at least the presumed consent of the rector of the church, unless the faculty has been restricted or taken away by the competent ordinary or unless express permission is required by particular law."

29 Cf. BNFPD, no. 86.

30   DMLPD, no. 26.

31   Ibid., no. 38.

32   Second Vatican Council, *Constitution on the Sacred Liturgy* (*Sacrosanctum Concilium*) (December 4, 1963) (Washington, D.C.: United States Catholic Conference, 1963), no. 10.

33   BNFPD, no. 5.

34   LG, no. 29, cited in PDO.

35   SC, no. 14.

36   STVI, pp. 51-57.

37   ADUS.

38   Ibid.

39   DMLPD, no. 39.

40   BNFPD, no. 5.

41   Acts 6:1-7.

42   Cf. Jn 13:1-15.

43   PDG (1984), no. 43.

44   BNFPD, no. 10.

45   Roman Pontifical, Ordination of Deacons, no. 199, in *Rites of Ordination of a Bishop, of Priests, and of Deacons* (Washington, D.C.: USCCB, 2003); cf. Mt 25:21.

CHAPTER TWO

THE MINISTRY AND LIFE OF DEACONS

I. The Relationships of the Deacon

Relationship with the Diocesan Bishop

41.   The deacon exercises his ministry within a specific pastoral context—the communion and mission of a diocesan Church.[1] He is in direct relationship with the diocesan bishop with whom he is in communion and under whose authority he exercises his ministry. In making his promise of respect and obedience to his bishop, the deacon takes as his model Christ, who became the servant of his Father. The diocesan bishop also enters into a relationship with the deacon since the deacon is his collaborator in the service of God's People. It is, therefore, a particular responsibility of the bishop to provide for the pastoral care of the deacons of his diocese. The bishop discharges this responsibility both personally and through the director of deacon personnel.[2]

Respect and obedience

42.   The bishop appoints the deacon to a specific assignment normally by means of an official letter of appointment.[3] The principal criteria for the assignment are the pastoral needs of the diocesan Church and the personal qualifications of the deacon, as these have been discerned in his previous experience and the course of his formation. The assignment also acknowledges the deacon's family and occupational responsibilities.

The bishop appoints the deacon to a specific ministry

43.   The bishop promotes "a suitable catechesis" throughout the diocesan Church to assist the lay faithful, religious, and clergy to have a richer and firmer sense about the deacon's identity, function, and role within the Church's ministry.[4] In fact, such a catechesis is also "an opportunity for the bishop, priests, religious, and laity to discern the needs and challenges of the local Church, to consider the types of services needed in order to meet them, to tailor a diaconal program to address them, and to begin the process of considering which men in the church might be called upon to undertake diaconal ministry."[5]

Suitable catechesis: An opportunity to discern needs, suitable nominees, and placement on the diocesan level

Letter of appointment

44.   The assignment of a deacon to a specific ministry, the delineation of his duties and responsibilities, and the designation of his immediate pastor or pastoral supervisor, who must be a priest, should always be clearly stated in the letter of appointment signed by the diocesan bishop. This document should make as explicit as possible the implicit expectations of the participants, thereby establishing a clear line of mutual responsibility and accountability among them. The director of deacon personnel, together with the deacon's designated pastor or priest supervisor (if the deacon is assigned to an office or agency not directed by a priest), a representative of that office or agency, and the deacon are to be involved in the preparation of the letter of appointment. "For the good of the deacon and to prevent improvisation, ordination should be accompanied by clear investiture of pastoral responsibility."[6] Although the wife of a married deacon has already given her permission before her husband's ordination to the demands of the diaconal ministry, nevertheless she should be "kept duly informed of [her husband's] activities in order to arrive at an harmonious balance between family, professional and ecclesial responsibilities."[7] Until the letter of appointment is signed by the bishop and publicly announced by the bishop's office, all parties are bound to confidentiality.

Rights and duties

45.   The diocesan bishop also ensures that the "rights and duties as foreseen by canons 273-283 of the *Code of Canon Law* with regard to clerics in general and deacons in particular"[8] are promoted.

Concerns for the newly ordained deacons

46.   The transition from candidate formation into an active diaconal ministry requires sensitivity. "Introducing the deacon to those in charge of the community (the parish priest, priests), and the community to the deacon, helps them not only to come to know each other but contributes to a collaboration based on mutual respect and dialogue, in a spirit of faith and fraternal charity."[9] Newly ordained deacons, therefore, are to be appointed to and supervised by a priest. This pastoral care of a newly ordained deacon, coordinated by the director of deacon personnel, extends for the first three years after ordination. This time would include opportunities for ongoing formation, with an initial emphasis upon the issues and concerns voiced by the newly ordained as he gains ministerial experience. It is likewise a unique opportunity to assist the deacon's family as it begins to adjust to its new situation within the community.

47.   With the approval of the diocesan bishop, a realistic program for the continuing education and formation of each deacon and the entire diaconal community should be designed "taking due account of factors such as age and circumstances of deacons, together with the demands made on them by their pastoral ministry."[10] The preparation, implementation, and evaluation of this program are to be coordinated by the director of deacon personnel. "In addition to the [continuing] formation offered to [all] deacons, special courses and initiatives should be arranged for those deacons who are married," including the participation of their wives and families, "where opportune. . . . However, [care must be given] to maintain the essential distinction of roles and the clear independence of the ministry."[11] Similarly, special initiatives in continuing formation should be arranged for deacons who are not married.

Continuing formation and education

Relationship with the Diocese

48.   While assuming different forms of diaconal ministry, a deacon exercises his service in both a diocesan setting and in an individual assignment. Therefore, he may be given specific responsibility, if he meets the necessary requirements, in an administrative position at a diocesan or parochial level.[12] However, in discharging these administrative responsibilities, "the deacon should recall that every action in the Church should be informed by charity and service to all. . . . Those deacons who are called to exercise such offices should be placed so as to discharge duties which are proper to the diaconate, in order to preserve the integrity of the diaconal ministry."[13]

Every diaconal service is informed by charity and service

49.   Deacons who possess the necessary requirements, experience, and talent may be appointed members of the diocesan pastoral council, finance council, or commissions. They may be assigned to diocesan pastoral work in specific social contexts: e.g., the pastoral care of the family or the pastoral needs of ethnic minorities.[14] They may also participate in a diocesan synod.[15] They may exercise the offices of chancellor, judge, assessor, auditor, promoter of justice, defender of the bond, and notary or may serve as the diocesan finance officer.[16] However, deacons do not "act as members of the council of priests, since this body exclusively represents the presbyterate."[17] Deacons may not "be constituted judicial vicars, adjunct judicial vicars, or vicars forane, since these offices are reserved for priests."[18] To strengthen the diaconal character of the diocesan

Diocesan appointments

Church, care is to be taken, therefore, to include, as much as possible, a diaconal presence within diocesan structures, as well as within parish communities.[19] Deacons who have parochial administrative training and experience may be entrusted, under a canonically appointed pastor or priest supervisor, to assist in the pastoral care of a parish or to temporarily guide a parish that lacks, because of a shortage, the immediate benefit of a resident pastor.[20] In these extraordinary situations, deacons "always have precedence over the non-ordained faithful," and their authority and responsibility "should always be clearly specified in writing when they are assigned office."[21]

Relationship with the Priesthood

Complementary ministries

50.   Deacons exercise their ministry in communion not only with their bishop but also with the priests who serve the diocesan Church. As collaborators in ministry, priests and deacons are two complementary but subordinate participants in the one apostolic ministry bestowed by Christ upon the apostles and their successors. The diaconate is not an abridged or substitute form of the priesthood, but is a full order in its own right.[22] Permanent deacons ought to foster fraternal bonds with transitional deacons. Through formal contacts arranged by the diocesan diaconate and vocation offices with the seminary program, in collaborative diocesan and parochial ministries, and in opportunities for shared study and prayer, the Order of Deacons can more clearly be understood and appreciated among those to be ordained to the Order of Priests.

Pastoral care of a parish

51.   The diocesan bishop may assign a deacon to assist a priest entrusted with the pastoral care of one or several parishes.[23] Deacons who possess administrative experience and have received pastoral theological training also may be called to guide Christian communities that do not have the immediate benefit of a resident priest.[24] "While it is a duty of deacons to respect the office of parish priest and to work in communion with all who share in his pastoral care, they also have the right to be accepted and fully recognized by all."[25] When a deacon is entrusted to guide a parish community, "it is necessary to specify that the moderator of the parish is a priest and that he is its proper pastor. To him alone has been entrusted the *cura animarum*, in which he is assisted by the deacon."[26] "When deacons supply in places where there is a shortage of priests, they do so by

ecclesial mandate. . . . It is they who preside at [such] Sunday celebrations"[27] in the absence of the priest. In dioceses where parish pastoral councils are constituted, these deacons are members of such councils by law.[28]

52.   Deacons and priests, as ordained ministers, should develop a genuine respect for each other, witnessing to the communion and mission they share with one another and with the diocesan bishop in mutual service to the People of God.[29] To foster this communion, it is important for the diocese to offer opportunities annually for shared retreats, days of recollection, deanery meetings, continuing education study days, and mutual work on diocesan councils and commissions, as well as regularly scheduled occasions for socialization. Further, the Church's communion and mission "is realized not only by the ministers in virtue of the Sacrament of Orders but also by all the lay faithful."[30] Therefore, the bishop, priests, and deacons need to welcome, inspire, and form the lay faithful to participate in the communion and mission of the Church "because of their Baptismal state and their specific vocation."[31]

Witnesses to communion and mission

53.   Priests should be informed about the sacramental identity of the deacon. They also are to be aware of the nature of diaconal spirituality and the specific functions the deacons will perform within the diocesan Church.[32] Priests need to collaborate with the diocesan bishop in planning for the inclusion of deacons into the life and ministry of the diocesan Church. Pastors especially are involved in the presentation, selection, and assessment processes of aspirants and candidates. Priests must serve as spiritual directors and pastoral supervisors and may serve as members of the faculty. They are expected to catechize the people on the ordained vocation of the deacon and to actively seek out, with the assistance of the parish community, competent nominees for this ministry.[33]

Theological formation and collaboration of priests

Relationship Among Deacons and Those in Formation

54.   By virtue of their ordination, a sacramental fraternity unites deacons. They form a community that witnesses to Christ, the Deacon-Servant. "Each deacon should have a sense of being joined with his fellow deacons in a bond of charity, prayer, obedience to their bishops, ministerial zeal and collaboration."[34] Therefore, "with the permission of the bishop . . . it would be opportune for deacons

Sacramental fraternity

periodically to meet to discuss their ministry, exchange experiences, advance formation and encourage each other in fidelity."[35] Canonically, deacons may "form associations among themselves to promote their spiritual life, to carry out charitable and pious works and pursue other objectives which are consonant with their sacramental consecration and mission."[36] However, it must be noted that associations that form as pressure groups that could promote conflict with the bishop are completely irreconcilable with the clerical state.[37] It may be desirable, therefore, for the diocesan bishop to form a diocesan structure composed of a proportionate number of deacons to coordinate diaconal ministry and life within the diocese.[38] The diocesan bishop would serve as its president and approve its statutes.[39] Finally, the diaconal community should be, for those in the aspirant and candidate paths in formation, "a precious support in the discernment of their vocation, in human growth, in the initiation to the spiritual life, in theological study and pastoral experience."[40]

Relationship with Women and Men Religious

Deacons and religious: Collaborators in ministry

55.   Deacons ought to promote collaboration between themselves and women and men religious who also have dedicated their lives to the service of the Church. Pastoral sensitivity between deacons and religious should be carefully nurtured. Opportunities for dialogue among deacons and religious could serve the Church well in developing and maintaining mutual understanding and support of each other's unique vocation, each of which accomplishes in its own way the common mission of service to the Church.

Relationship with the Laity

Foster the mission of the faithful

56.   By ordination, deacons are members of the clergy.[41] The vast majority of deacons in the United States, married or celibate, have secular employment and do not engage exclusively in specific church-related ministries. This combination of an ordained minister with a secular occupation and personal and family obligations can be a great strength, opportunity, and witness to the laity on how they too might integrate their baptismal call and state in life in living their Christian faith in society.[42]

The Church: A communion of service

57.   The laity, as members of the Church, have an obligation and right to share in the communion and mission of the Church. Through his ordination to service, the deacon promotes, in an

active fashion, the various lay apostolates and guides these in communion with the bishop and local priests.[43] In collaboration with his bishop and the priests of his diocese, the deacon has a special role to promote communion and to counter the strong emphasis on individualism prevalent in the United States. Set aside for service, the deacon links together the individual and diverse segments of the community of believers. In his works of charity, the deacon guides and witnesses to the Church "the love of Christ for all men instead of personal interests and ideologies which are injurious to the universality of salvation . . . the *diakonia* of charity necessarily leads to a growth of communion within the particular Churches since charity is the very soul of ecclesial communion."[44]

Relationship with Society

58.   The diaconate is lived in a particularly powerful way in the manner in which a deacon fulfills his obligations to his secular occupation, to his civic and public responsibilities, and among his family and neighbors. This, in turn, enables the deacon to bring back to the Church an appreciation of the meaning and value of the Gospel as he discerns it in the lives and questions of the people he has encountered. In his preaching and teaching, the deacon articulates the needs and hopes of the people he has experienced, thereby animating, motivating, and facilitating a commitment among the lay faithful to an evangelical service in the world.[45]

Deacons must be involved in the world

59.   Specifically, in the third Christian millennium, "the whole Church is called to greater apostolic commitment which is both personal and communitarian, renewed and generous."[46] At the heart of this call is an awareness of a new evangelization: i.e., "to rekindle the faith in the Christian conscience of many and cause the joyful proclamation of salvation to resound in society."[47] The deacon, as herald of the Gospel, has an important pastoral responsibility in new evangelization.[48] Pope John Paul II reminds the Church that "what moves me even more strongly to proclaim the urgency of missionary evangelization is the fact that it is the primary service which the Church can render to every individual . . . in the modern world."[49] The deacon is ordained precisely for service in both the sanctuary and the marketplace.

The deacon and the new evangelization

Ministry-employment compatibility

60.   The secular employment of a deacon is also linked with his ministry.[50] Although his secular work may benefit the community, some professions can become incompatible with the pastoral responsibilities of his ministry. The bishop, "bearing in mind the requirements of ecclesial communion and of the fruitfulness of pastoral ministry, shall evaluate individual cases as they arise, [and may require] a change of profession after ordination."[51]

Unity in Pastoral Activity

Diocese-coordinated services

61.   Under the diocesan bishop's authority, joint meetings and cooperative action "arranged between priests, deacons, religious, and laity involved in pastoral work [can] avoid compartmentalization or the development of isolated groups and . . . guarantee coordinated unity for different pastoral activities."[52]

II. Diaconal Spirituality

Introduction

Jesus, the Servant

62.   The primary sources of a deacon's spirituality are his participation in the sacraments of Christian initiation, as well as his sacramental identity and participation in ordained ministry. For a deacon who is married, his spirituality is nurtured further in the Sacrament of Matrimony, which sanctifies conjugal love and constitutes it as a sign of the love with which Christ gives himself to the Church. For the celibate deacon, loving God and serving his neighbor roots his whole person in a total and undivided consecration to Christ. For each deacon, his model *par excellence* is Jesus Christ, the Servant, who lived totally at the service of his Father, for the good of every person.[53] To live their ministry to the fullest, "deacons must know Christ intimately so that He may shoulder the burdens of their ministry."[54]

Spiritual Life

The priority of the spiritual life

63.   Deacons are obligated to give priority to the spiritual life and to live their *diakonia* with generosity. They should integrate their family obligations, professional life, and ministerial responsibilities so as to grow in their commitment to the person and mission of Christ, the Servant. Clerics have a special obligation to seek holiness in their lives "because they are consecrated to God by a new title in the reception of orders as dispensers of God's mysteries in the service of His people."[55]

Simplicity of Life

64.   Deacons are charged at ordination to shape a way of life always according to the example of Christ and to imitate Christ who came not to be served but to serve. Therefore, deacons are called to a simple lifestyle. Simplicity of life enables a cleric "to stand beside the underprivileged, to practice solidarity with their efforts to create a more just society, to be more sensitive and capable of understanding and discerning realities involving the economic and social aspects of life, and to promote a preferential option for the poor."[56] The prophetic significance of this lifestyle, "so urgently needed in affluent and consumeristic societies,"[57] is its important witness in animating the *diakonia* of every Christian to serve "especially those who are poor or in any way afflicted."[58]

Simple lifestyle

Pastoral Service

65.   As Pope John Paul II observed, "a deeply felt need in the decision to reestablish the diaconate was and is that of a greater and more direct presence of Church ministers in the various spheres such as family, work, school, etc., in addition to existing pastoral structures."[59] While transforming the world is the proper role of the laity, the deacon—in communion with his bishop and the diocesan presbyterate—exhorts, consecrates, and guides the People of God in living faithfully the communion and mission they share in Christ, especially in making the Gospel visible in their daily lives through their concern for justice, peace, and respect for life.[60]

Engaged in the world

III. The Deacon in His State of Life

The Married Deacon

66.   The majority of deacons in the United States are married.[61] These men bring to the Sacrament of Holy Orders the gifts already received and still being nurtured through their participation in the Sacrament of Matrimony. This sacrament sanctifies the love of husbands and wives, making that love an efficacious sign of the love of Christ for his Church. Marriage requires an "interpersonal giving of self, a mutual fidelity, a source of [and openness to] new life, [and] a support in times of joy and sorrow."[62] Lived in faith, this ministry within the domestic Church is a sign to the entire Church of the love of Christ. It forms the basis of the married deacon's unique gift within the Church.[63]

Married love is a sign of the love of Christ for the Church

Family life, work,
and ministry

67.   "In particular the deacon and his wife must be a living example of fidelity and indissolubility in Christian marriage before a world which is in dire need of such signs. By facing in a spirit of faith the challenges of married life and the demands of daily living, they strengthen the family life not only of the Church community but of the whole of society. They also show how the obligations of family life, work and ministry can be harmonized in the service of the Church's mission. Deacons and their wives and children can be a great encouragement to others who are working to promote family life."[64]

Witness to the
sanctity of marriage

68.   A married deacon, with his wife and family, gives witness to the sanctity of marriage. The more they grow in mutual love, conforming their lives to the Church's teaching on marriage and sexuality, the more they give to the Christian community a model of Christ-like love, compassion, and self-sacrifice. The married deacon must always remember that through his sacramental participation in both vocational sacraments, first in Matrimony and again in Holy Orders, he is challenged to be faithful to both. With integrity he must live out both sacraments in harmony and balance. The wife of a deacon should be included with her husband, when appropriate, in diocesan clergy and parochial staff gatherings. A deacon and his wife, both as a spiritual man and woman and as a couple, have much to share with the bishop and his priests about the Sacrament of Matrimony. A diaconal family also brings a unique presence and understanding of the domestic family. "By facing in a spirit of faith the challenges of married life and the demands of daily living, [the married deacon and his family] strengthen the family life not only of the Church community but of the whole of society."[65]

The Celibate Deacon

Celibacy: Consecration
to Christ with an
undivided heart

69.   The Church acknowledges the gift of celibacy that God grants to certain of its members who wholeheartedly live it "*according to its true nature* and according to its real purposes, that is for evangelical, spiritual and pastoral motives."[66] The essential meaning of celibacy is grounded in Jesus' preaching of the kingdom of God. Its deepest source is love of Christ and dedication to his mission. "In celibate life, indeed, love becomes a sign of total and undivided consecration to Christ and of greater freedom to serve God and man. The choice of celibacy is not an expression of contempt for marriage nor of flight from reality but a special way of serving man and the world."[67]

70.   The celibate commitment remains one of the most fundamental expressions of Jesus' call to radical discipleship for the sake of
the kingdom on earth and as an eschatological sign of the kingdom of
heaven.[68] "This perfect continency, out of desire for the kingdom of
heaven, has always been held in particular honor in the Church. The
reason for this was and is that perfect continency for the love of God
is an incentive to charity, and is certainly a particular source of spiritual fecundity in the world."[69]

71.   If the celibate deacon gives up one kind of family, he gains
another. In Christ, the people he serves become mother, brother, and
sister. In this way, celibacy as a sign and motive of pastoral charity
takes flesh. Reciprocity, mutuality, and affection shared with many
become channels that mold and shape the celibate deacon's pastoral
love and his sexuality. "Celibacy should not be considered just as a
legal norm . . . but rather as a value . . . whereby [the celibate dea-
con] takes on the likeness of Jesus Christ . . . as a full and joyful
availability in his heart for the pastoral ministry."[70]

Celibacy Affects Every Deacon

72.   In one way or another, celibacy affects every deacon, married
or unmarried. Understanding the nature of celibacy—its value and
its practice—are essential to the married deacon. Not only does this
understanding strengthen and nurture his own commitment to mar-
ital chastity, but it also helps to prepare him for the possibility of living celibate chastity should his wife predecease him. This concern is
particularly unique within the diaconate. Tragically, some deacons
who were married at the time of ordination only begin to face the
issues involved with celibacy upon the death of their wives. As difficult as this process is, all deacons need to appreciate the impact
celibacy can have on their lives and ministry.

The Widowed Deacon

73.   The death of a married deacon's wife is a "particular moment
in life which calls for faith and Christian hope."[71] The death of the wife
of a married deacon introduces a new reality into the daily routine of
his family and ministry. Charity should be extended to the widowed
deacon as he assesses and accepts his new personal circumstances, so
he will not neglect his primary duty as father to his children or any new
needs his family might have.[72] As required, a widowed deacon should

be assisted to seek professional counsel and spiritual direction as he encounters and integrates the bereavement process. Further, the fraternal closeness of his bishop, the priests with whom he ministers, and the diaconal community should offer comfort and reassurance in this special moment in his life.[73] This adjustment to a new state of life can be achieved only in time through prayer, counsel, and an "intensification of one's dedication to others for the love of God in the ministry."[74]

Ministry to a deacon's widow

74.   A similar sensitivity also should be given to the widow of a deacon since she shared so intimately in her husband's life and ministerial witness. The bishop and her pastor, as well as the diaconal and parish communities, should extend appropriate and adequate support in her bereavement. Widows of deacons ought to remain connected with the diaconal community, not only because of support and encouragement, but because of the unique bonds that had been forged by virtue of her husband's ordination.

Dispensations for remarriage or from the obligations of the clerical state

75.   In exceptional cases, the Holy See may grant a dispensation for a new marriage[75] or for a release from the obligations of the clerical state. However, to ensure a mature decision in discerning God's will, effective pastoral care should be provided to maintain that a proper and sufficient period of time has elapsed before either of these dispensations is sought. If a dispensation for a new marriage is petitioned and granted, additional time will be required for the formation of a stable relationship in the new marriage, as well as the enabling of his new wife to obtain sufficient understanding and experience about the diaconate in order to give her written, informed consent and support.

A Deacon and Family Confronting Divorce

Pastoral care of a divorced deacon and his family

76.   Divorce between a deacon and his wife can happen. In this situation, suitable pastoral care should be offered to the deacon, his wife, and their children. This pastoral care, which may be facilitated by the director of deacon personnel or any other qualified person on behalf of the bishop, should include ample time to work through the various stages of grieving and adjustment caused by divorce. The determination of the divorced deacon's ministerial status will require sensitivity and prudence on the part of the bishop, the pastor or pastoral supervisor, the ministerial community, and other

institutions in which the deacon serves. Members of the diaconal community are also in a unique position to reach out, as appropriate, in order to help the divorced couple and family deal with the challenges the divorce may entail.

IV. The Permanency of the Order of Deacons

77.   Underlying the restoration and renewal of the diaconate at the Second Vatican Council was the principle that the diaconate is a stable and permanent rank of ordained ministry. Since the history of the order over the last millennium, however, has been centered on the diaconate as a transitory stage leading to the priesthood, actions that may obfuscate the stability and permanence of the order should be minimized. This would include the ordination of celibate or widowed deacons to the priesthood. "Hence ordination [of a permanent deacon] to the Priesthood . . . must always be a very rare exception, and only for special and grave reasons . . . Given the exceptional nature of such cases, the diocesan bishop should consult the Congregation for Catholic Education with regard to the intellectual and theological preparation of the candidate, and also the Congregation for the Clergy concerning the program of priestly formation and the aptitude of the candidate to the priestly ministry."[76]

Order of Deacons: Permanent and stable

V. The Obligations and Rights of Deacons

Incardination
78.   "Through the imposition of hands and the prayer of consecration, [the deacon] is constituted a sacred minister and a member of the hierarchy."[77] Having already clearly expressed in writing his intention to serve the diocesan Church for life, upon his ordination the deacon is incardinated into the diocesan Church. "Incardination is a juridical bond. It has ecclesiastical and spiritual significance in as much as it expresses the ministerial dedication of the deacon to a specific diocesan Church."[78]

Incardination: A juridical bond

The Church's Ministry of the Word
79.   As a participant in the Church's ministry of the word, the deacon heeds the charge given him at ordination: "Receive the Gospel of Christ, whose herald you now are. Believe what you read, teach what you believe, and practice what you teach."[79] The deacon

"Receive the Gospel of Christ, whose herald you now are."

must always remain a student of God's word, for only when the word is deeply rooted in his own life can he bring that word to others.[80] The deacon ought to remember that since he is a member of the hierarchy, his actions and public pronouncements involve the Church and its Magisterium. Therefore, he is obligated to cherish the communion and mission that bind him to the Holy Father and his own bishop, especially in his preaching of the Scriptures, the Creed, Catholic teachings, and the disciplines of the Church.[81]

The *diakonia* of the Word
80.   Deacons are ordained "to proclaim the Gospel and preach the Word of God."[82] They "have the faculty to preach everywhere, in accordance with the conditions established by [Canon Law]."[83] "Deacons should be trained carefully to prepare their homilies in prayer, in study of the sacred texts, in perfect harmony with the Magisterium and in keeping with the [age, culture, and abilities] of those to whom they preach."[84] Further, "by their conduct . . . by transmitting Christian doctrine and by devoting attention to the problems of our time . . . [deacons] collaborate with the bishop and the priests in the exercise of a ministry which is not of their wisdom but of the Word of God, calling all to conversion and holiness."[85]

Publication, use of public media, and the Internet
81.   Deacons are obliged to obtain the permission of their bishop before submitting for publication written material concerning faith and morals. Deacons are required to adhere to the norms established by the United States Conference of Catholic Bishops or diocesan policies when participating in radio or television broadcasts, public media, and the Internet.[86]

The Church's Ministry of Liturgy

The *diakonia* of the liturgy
82.   As an ordained participant in the Church's ministry of liturgy, the deacon confirms his identity as servant of the Body of Christ. In the celebration of the sacraments, whether he serves as a presider or assists the presider, "let him remember that, when lived with faith and reverence, these actions of the Church contribute much to growth in the spiritual life and to the increase of the Christian community."[87]

83.   Deacons, in hierarchical communion with the bishop and priests, serve in the sanctification of the Christian community. "In the Eucharistic Sacrifice, the deacon does not celebrate the mystery: rather, he effectively represents on the one hand, the people of God

and, specifically, helps them to unite their lives to the offering of Christ; while on the other, in the name of Christ himself, he helps the Church to participate in the fruits of that sacrifice."[88] While exercising his liturgical ministries, "the deacon is to observe faithfully the rubrics of the liturgical books without adding, omitting or changing of his own volition what they require. . . . For the Sacred Liturgy they should vest worthily and with dignity, in accordance with the prescribed liturgical norms. The dalmatic, in its appropriate liturgical colors, together with the alb, cincture and stole, 'constitutes the liturgical dress proper to deacons.'"[89] Specific liturgical functions of the deacon in the Latin rite of the Catholic Church are contained in Chapter One of this *Directory*.

The Church's Ministry of Charity and Justice

84.   As an ordained participant in the Church's ministry of charity and justice, the deacon assumes the duties entrusted to him by his bishop with humility and enthusiasm. At the core of his spirituality, a deacon puts on Christ and is guided by the love of Christ in caring for all in his charge: "Charity is the very soul of ecclesial communion."[90]

The *diakonia* of charity

85.   In the prayer of diaconal ordination, the bishop implores God that the deacon may be "full of all the virtues, sincere in charity, solicitous towards the weak and the poor, humble in their service . . . [and] may . . . be the image of your Son who did not come to be served but to serve."[91] Therefore, "by word and example," the deacon places himself "at the constant service of [his] brothers and sisters."[92] This service will include diocesan and parochial works of charity, including the Church's concern for social justice. It will also extend into Christian formation—working with youth and adults in promoting justice and life in all its phases—transforming the world through personal witness in conformity with the Gospel of life and justice. The deacon must strive, therefore, to serve all of humanity "without discrimination, while devoting particular care to the suffering and the sinful."[93] Ultimately, the deacon's principal *diakonia*— a sign of the Church's mission—"should bring [all whom he serves] to an experience of God's love and move [them] to conversion by opening [their] heart[s] to the work of grace."[94]

VI. United States Conference of Catholic Bishops: Particular Law Governing Deacons in the United States

86.   A number of practical concerns have emerged regarding diaconal ministry. Because of the diverse responses that exist throughout the United States, the United States Conference of Catholic Bishops has published the following *particular law* to provide a more harmonious approach.

Age for Ordination

87.   In accord with Canon Law, the United States Conference of Catholic Bishops establishes the minimum age for ordination to the permanent diaconate at thirty-five for all candidates, married or celibate. The establishment of a maximum age for ordination is at the discretion of the diocesan bishop, keeping in mind the particular needs and expectations of the diocese regarding diaconal ministry and life.

Clerical Title

88.   While various forms of address have emerged with regard to deacons, the Congregation for the Clergy has determined that in all forms of address for permanent deacons, the appropriate title is "Deacon."[95]

Clerical Attire

89.   The Code of Canon Law does not oblige permanent deacons to wear an ecclesiastical garb.[96] Further, because they are prominent and active in secular professions and society, the United States Conference of Catholic Bishops specifies that permanent deacons should resemble the lay faithful in dress and matters of lifestyle. Each diocesan bishop should, however, determine and promulgate any exceptions to this law, as well as specify the appropriate clerical attire if it is to be worn.[97]

Liturgy of the Hours

90.   Permanent deacons are required to include as part of their daily prayer those parts of the Liturgy of the Hours known as Morning and Evening Prayer. Permanent deacons are obliged to pray for the universal Church. Whenever possible, they should lead these prayers with the community to whom they have been assigned to minister.

Participation in Political Office

91.   A permanent deacon may not present his name for election to any public office or in any other general election, or accept a nomination or an appointment to public office, without the prior written permission of the diocesan bishop.[98] A permanent deacon may not actively and publicly participate in another's political campaign without the prior written permission of the diocesan bishop.

Temporary Absence from an Assignment

92.   Permanent deacons may temporarily absent themselves from their place of assignment with the permission of their proper pastor or priest supervisor.

Decree of Appointment

93.   A deacon shall receive a decree of appointment from his bishop, which should delineate his specific duties and responsibilities and the designation of his proper pastor or priest supervisor.[99]

Support of the Clergy

94.   Permanent deacons are to take care of their own and their family's needs using income derived from their full-time employment by the diocese, parish, or secular profession. In an individual situation of need, the diocesan Church ought to assist the deacon and his family in charity.

Social Security Insurance

95.   To provide for their own upkeep, every permanent deacon is obliged to satisfy the legal requirements for Social Security benefits or a comparable program.[100]

Remuneration

96.   (1) Permanent deacons in full-time employment by the diocese, parish, or agency are to receive remuneration commensurate with the salaries and benefits provided to the lay men and women on staff for that particular occupation.[101]

(2) Permanent deacons in full-time secular employment, as well as those in part-time ministries, are to be reimbursed for legitimate expenses incurred in their ministry.[102]

Continuing Formation and Spiritual Retreat

97.   Deacons are entitled to a period of time each year for continuing education and spiritual retreat. Norms should be established in each diocese regarding suitable length of time for these activities and the manner in which the deacon shall receive financial assistance for his expenses either from the diocese, from the current place of ministerial service, or from a combination of sources.

Financial Assistance to Those in Formation

98.   The diocesan bishop is to determine the financial assistance, if any, that is to be provided to inquirers, as well as those enrolled in the aspirant path in diaconal formation. For those admitted into the candidate path in formation for the diaconate, some provision for financial assistance, at least partial, should be provided for educational needs (e.g., tuition, books, tapes) and for mandatory aspects of formation (e.g., required retreats, workshops).

Loss of Diaconal Status

99.   A deacon can be returned to the lay state by canonical dismissal or because of a dispensation granted by the Holy See. Once dismissed or dispensed, he no longer enjoys any rights or privileges accorded clerics by the law of the Church.[103] Any responsibility, financial or liability, ceases on the part of the diocese.

Withdrawal of Diaconal Faculties

100.   Bishops are reminded that if the ministry of a permanent deacon becomes ineffective or even harmful due to some personal difficulties or irresponsible behavior, his ministerial assignment and faculties are to be withdrawn by the diocesan bishop in accord with Canon Law.

Diocesan Liability

101.   The diocesan bishop should provide for insurance regarding the liability of the diocese for actions taken by a permanent deacon in the course of his public official ministry. The same policies that govern liability for priests in the diocese should be applicable to permanent deacons.

Service of a Deacon from Another Diocesan Church

102.   A diocesan bishop is under no obligation to accept a permanent deacon—ordained or incardinated elsewhere—for assignment

to a diocesan or parochial ministry. Nevertheless, since a permanent deacon is an ordained cleric, the bishop may not ordinarily forbid a visiting permanent deacon the exercise of his order provided that the deacon is not under censure.

Bi-Ritual Permanent Deacons

When a permanent deacon of the Eastern Catholic Churches is granted bi-ritual faculties to assist in the Roman Church, the theological understanding of the sacraments and the order of the diaconate in the Eastern Catholic Churches is to be respected. Practically, a deacon of the Eastern Catholic Churches is not to be allowed to solemnize marriages in the Roman Church.

Resignation and Retirement

103.   Norms should be established in each diocese regarding the age, health, and other matters that need to be considered regarding a deacon's resignation from a ministerial office or his retirement from ministerial duties.

NORMS

(The number[s] found in parentheses after each norm refer[s] to the appropriate paragraph[s] in this *Directory*.)

1.   It is incumbent on the bishop to provide for the pastoral care of deacons of the diocese. This is discharged personally and through the director of deacon personnel, who must always be a cleric. (41)
2.   The principal criteria for the assignment of a deacon are the pastoral needs of the diocesan Church and the personal qualifications of the deacon, as these have been discerned in his previous experience and the course of his formation. (42)
3.   A catechetical introduction for priests, religious, and laity to the diaconate at the time of its restoration and throughout its development in the diocese should be planned and well implemented. (43, 53)
4.   Deacon assignments ought to provide ample opportunities for an integrated exercise of the threefold diaconal ministry: word, liturgy, and charity. (44)
5.   A program for newly ordained deacons during the first three years of their ministry is to be coordinated and supervised by

the director of deacon personnel. (46) Under the bishop's authority, periodic meetings should be arranged between priests, deacons, religious, and laity involved in pastoral work "to avoid compartmentalization or the development of isolated groups and to guarantee coordinated unity for different pastoral activities in the diocese."[104] (61)

6. The deacon must give priority to the spiritual life. As minister of liturgy, the deacon confirms his identity as servant of the Body of Christ. (63, 82)

7. The vocation to the permanent diaconate presupposes the stability and permanency of the order. Hence, the ordination of a permanent deacon to the priesthood is always a rare exception, and must be done in consultation with the Congregation for Catholic Education and the Congregation for the Clergy. (77)

8. Deacons have the faculty to preach everywhere, in accordance with the conditions established by law. (80)

9. Deacons are obliged to obtain the permission of their bishop before submitting for publication written materials concerning faith and morals. They are to adhere to the norms established by the United States Conference of Catholic Bishops, or diocesan policies, in publicly representing the Church. (81)

10. The minimum age for ordination to the permanent diaconate is thirty-five. The establishment of a maximum age of ordination is at the discretion of the diocesan bishop, keeping in mind both diocesan needs and expectations of diaconal life and ministry. (87)

11. In all forms of address for permanent deacons, "Deacon" is preferred. (88)

12. The *Code of Canon Law* does not oblige permanent deacons to wear an ecclesiastical garb. Further, because they are more prominent and active in secular professions and society, the United States Conference of Catholic Bishops specifies that permanent deacons should resemble the lay faithful in dress and matters of lifestyle. Each ordinary should, however, determine and promulgate any exceptions to this law, as well as specify the appropriate clerical attire. (89)

13. Permanent deacons are required to include as part of their daily prayer those parts of the Liturgy of the Hours known as Morning and Evening Prayer. (90)

14. A permanent deacon may not present his name for election to any public office or in any other general election, or accept a

nomination or an appointment to public office, without the prior written permission of the diocesan bishop. A permanent deacon may not actively and publicly participate in another's political campaign without the prior written permission of the diocesan bishop. (91)

15. The deacon shall receive an official letter of appointment from his bishop. (44, 45, 93)

16. Until the decree of appointment is publicly announced by the bishop's office, all parties are bound to confidentiality. (44)

17. Every permanent deacon is obliged to satisfy the legal requirements of Social Security benefits or a comparable program. (95)

18. Deacons in full-time employment by the diocese or parish are to receive remuneration commensurate with the salaries and benefits provided to the lay men or women on staff for that particular occupation. (96)

19. Deacons in full-time secular employment, as well as those in part-time ministries, are to be reimbursed for legitimate expenses incurred in their ministry. (96)

20. For those admitted into the candidate path in formation, some provision for financial assistance should be provided for educational needs and mandatory aspects of formation. (98)

21. The diocesan bishop should provide for insurance regarding the liability of the diocese for actions taken by a permanent deacon in the course of his public official ministry. The same policies that govern liability for priests in the diocese should be applicable to permanent deacons. (101)

22. Norms should be established in each diocese regarding the age, health, and other matters that need to be considered regarding a deacon's resignation from a ministerial office or his retirement from ministerial duties. (103)

NOTES

1   DMLPD, nos. 1-2.

2   Ibid., nos. 8, 78, 80; cf. no. 3.

3   Cf. CIC, cc. 156, 157. DMLPD, no. 8, refers to this written conferral of office as a "decree of appointment." Cf. also "Appendix: Sample Documents," in *Clergy Procedural Handbook*, Randolph R. Calvo and Nevin J. Klinger, eds. (Washington, D.C.: Canon Law Society of America, 1992), 128ff, for examples of possible formulations of the letter of appointment.

4   BNFPD, no. 16.

5   PDG (1984), no. 51.

6   DMLPD, no. 40; cf., also, Ibid., no. 41. "The decree of appointment should specify the ministry of the deacon. A subsequent 'ministerial agreement' should not be necessary, nor should it be signed by the deacon's wife: this is [a] blurring of the lines of ministry and authority." Congregation for Catholic Education and the Congregation for the Clergy, *Joint Study of the US Draft Document—National Directory for the Formation, Ministry and Life of Permanent Deacons in the United States*, Prot. No. 78/2000 (March 4, 2002). Given the comprehensive nature of the information to be provided in the bishops' letter of appointment, the information that was formerly developed as a separate "ministerial agreement" may now be done as an integral part of the preparation of the bishop's letter of appointment.

7   DMLPD, no. 61.

8   Ibid., no. 7.

9   Ibid., no. 77.

10   Ibid., nos. 78-79.

11   Ibid., no. 81. Cf., also, no. 60, regarding the needs of celibate deacons.

12   Ibid., no. 41.

13   Ibid., no. 42.

14   Ibid.

15   Ibid.

16   Ibid., nos. 42, 38.

17   Ibid., no. 42.

18   Ibid.

19   Ibid., nos. 41-42.

20   Ibid., nos. 40-42.

21   Ibid., no. 41.

22   Ibid., no. 1, 41.

23   CIC, cc. 519, 517:1.

24   Ibid., no. 517:2; DMLPD, no. 41.

25   DMLPD, no. 41.

26   Ibid.

27   Ibid.

28   Ibid., no. 41; cf. CIC, c. 536.

29   Ibid.; cf. no. 37.

30   Pope John Paul II, *On the Vocation and the Mission of the Lay Faithful in the Church and in the World* (*Christifideles Laici*) (December 30, 1988) (Washington, D.C.: United States Catholic Conference, 1988), no. 23.

31   Ibid.

32   BNFPD, no. 90: "Ordinaries . . . to whom the present document is given, [should] ensure that it becomes an object of attentive reflection in communion with their priests and communities."

33   Ibid., no. 16.

34   DMLPD, no. 6.

35   Ibid., no. 6.

36   Ibid., no. 11.

37   Ibid.

38   Ibid., no. 80.

39   Ibid.

40   BNFPD, no. 26.

41   DMLPD, nos. 1, 7.

42   Ibid., no. 73.

43   Cf. Pope John Paul II, General Audience, *Deacons Have Many Pastoral Functions* (October 13, 1993), no. 5.

44   DMLPD, no. 55.

45   Ibid., no. 43; cf. nos. 25-27.

46   Congregation for the Clergy, *The Priest and the Third Christian Millennium* (March 19, 1999), (Washington, D.C.: United States Catholic Conference, 1999) Introduction.

47   Ibid.

48   DMLPD, no. 26.

49   Pope John Paul II, Encyclical Letter, *On the Permanent Validity of the Church's Missionary Mandate* (*Redemptoris Missio*) (December 7, 1990) (Washington, D.C.: United States Catholic Conference, 1990), no. 2.

50   DMLPD, no. 12.

51   Ibid.

52   Ibid., no. 78.

53   BNFPD, no. 11.

54   DMLPD, no. 50.

55   CIC, c. 276:1.

56   PDV, no. 30.

57   Ibid.

58   GS, no. 1.

59   Pope John Paul II, General Audience, *Deacons Serve the Kingdom of God* (October 5, 1993), no. 6.

60   ADUS.

61   NSD (1996) reports that 97 percent of all deacons in the United States are married (p. 2).

62   DMLPD, no. 61.

63   Ibid.

64   ADUS.

65   Ibid.

66   PDV, no. 50.

67   DMLPD, no. 60.

68   LG, no. 42.

69   Ibid.; cf. *The Roman Pontifical* (Washington, D.C.: International Commission on English in the Liturgy, 1978).

70   PDV, no. 50.

71   DMLPD, no. 62.

72   Ibid.

73   Ibid.

74   Ibid.

75   DMLPD, Note 193, citing Congregation for Divine Worship and the Discipline of the Sacraments, Circular Letter, Prot. No. 263/97 (June 6, 1997), no. 8.

76   Ibid., no. 5.

77   Ibid., no. 1.

78   Ibid., no. 2; cf. Bishops'Committee on the Diaconate, National Conference of Catholic Bishops, *Protocol for the Incardination/Excardination of Permanent Deacons* (1995, revised 1999).

79   The Roman Pontifical, op. cit., Ordination of Deacons, p. 171.

80   St. Augustine, *Serm.* 179, no. 1.

81   DMLPD, no. 23.

82   Ibid., no. 24.

83   Ibid.; cf. CIC, c. 764.

84   Ibid., no. 25.

85   Ibid., no. 23.

86   Ibid., no. 26.

87   Ibid., no. 53.

88   Ibid., no. 28.

89   Ibid., no. 30.

90   Ibid., no. 55.

91   Ibid., no. 38, citing *Pontificale Romanum-De Ordinatione Episcopi, Presbyterorum et Diaconorum*, no. 207, p. 122.

92   Ibid, no. 38.

93   Ibid.

94   Ibid.

95   "The introduction of the title 'Reverend Mr.' for permanent deacons could further complicate the issue of identity for deacons. The term 'Reverend' has traditionally been associated with priests and used only for transitional deacons on their way to priesthood. As there is great sensitivity surrounding the issue of a deacon being seen as a 'mini-priest,' it would seem that the title 'Reverend Mr.' would lead to continued identification of the diaconate with the priesthood, rather than contributing to the independence and integrity of the Order of Deacon in itself. The title 'Deacon' would, of course, be appropriate." Congregation for Catholic Education and the Congregation for the Clergy, *Joint Study of the US Draft Document—National Directory for the Formation, Ministry and Life of Permanent Deacons in the United States*, Prot. No. 78/2000 (March 4, 2002).

96   CIC, c. 288.

97   Liturgical books clearly specify the liturgical garb of a deacon for various rites and liturgical celebrations. Here, the intent is to bring about harmony between dioceses, especially on a provincial level, as to the appropriate clerical attire, if any, for other formal clerical ministries of deacons. In some places, deacons wear a clerical shirt and Roman collar; others wear pectoral crosses or deacon lapel pins, while still others wear a modified dress shirt. There is confusion about what is appropriate clerical attire among deacons themselves and among the lay faithful. Recognizing the geographical and social diversity that exists in our country, the Bishops' Committee on the Diaconate offers this particular law as a practical response to a national concern.

98   DMLPD, no. 13. The rationale is that the identity of a political candidate becomes well known and any investigation regarding background or reputation of the permanent deacon should be the responsibility of ecclesial authorities so as to avoid any undue or unwarranted publicity in the public media. In making his determination to grant written permission, the bishop should investigate the background of the permanent deacon, including his many social relationships (e.g., memberships in clubs, organizations) so that nothing would become an embarrassment to the Church. The bishop should investigate the credit rating of the deacon so that there is no question of unreasonable indebtedness. He also should be concerned about fundraising that the permanent deacon, as a political candidate, will have to initiate, as well as improper reflections that might occur by associating the deacon, as a political candidate, with a particular party and its platform.

99   Ibid., no. 41; cf. no. 40.

100   Ibid., no. 15; cf. CIC, cc. 281, 1274.

101   Ibid., no. 16.

102   Ibid, no. 20. Examples include videos for baptismal preparation programs, handouts, refreshments for required gatherings, and distinctive clerical garb. It also could include reimbursement for the personal use of and gas for his car in ministry, using IRS mileage standards and records.

103   Ibid., no. 21; cf. CIC, cc. 290-293.

104   DMLPD, no. 78.

CHAPTER THREE

DIMENSIONS IN THE FORMATION OF DEACONS

I. Introduction

104.   There are three separate but integral paths that constitute a unified diocesan formation program for deacons: aspirant, candidate, and post-ordination. Although this *Directory* addresses each path separately, they nevertheless become "one sole organic journey" in diaconal formation.[1] In each path, the four dimensions or specific areas in formation—human, spiritual, intellectual, and pastoral—are always essential.[2]

Separate paths: A unified formation program

II. Dimensions in Formation

105.   One who will serve as a deacon requires a formation that promotes the development of the whole person. Therefore, the four dimensions in formation should be so interrelated as to achieve a continual integration of their objectives in the life of each participant and in his exercise of ministry.

Four dimensions in ministerial formation

Human Dimension

106.   A participant comes to formation with a history of interrelationships with other people. Formation for ministry begins with human formation and development. Participants "should therefore cultivate a series of human qualities, not only out of proper and due growth and realization of self, but also with a view to the ministry."[3]

Growth in self-formation

OBJECTIVES

107.   Deacons have an important role in the field of human development and the promotion of justice. Because of their close living and working situations in society, they can well understand, interpret, and try to bring solutions to personal and social problems in the light of the Gospel. Therefore, deacons need to be close to the people, helping them to understand the realities of social life so they can try to improve it. Deacons should have the courage to speak out

Cultivate qualities with a view to diaconal ministry

for the weak and defend their rights. As a prophetic voice for the needs of others, the deacon proclaims God's word in the contemporary world. In this evangelizing role, the deacon collaborates with the diocesan bishop in the latter's responsibility for catechesis in the local Church.[4] The Congregation for the Evangelization of Peoples, in its *Guide for Catechists*, offers the following attributes for catechists that apply equally to deacons:

a. on the purely human sphere: psychophysical equilibrium—good health, sense of responsibility, honesty, and dynamism; good professional and family conduct, spirit of sacrifice, strength, perseverance . . .;

b. with a view to the functions of a [deacon]: good human relations, a good ability to dialogue with those of other religions, grasp of one's culture, ability to communicate, willingness to work with others, leadership qualities, balance judgment, openness of mind, a sense of realism, a capacity to transmit consolation and hope . . .;

c. with a view to particular situations or roles: aptitudes for working in the fields of peacemaking, development, socio-cultural promotion, justice, health care. . . .[5]

To this list may be added other important qualities, such as the ability to manage conflict, collaborate, and organize.

Four aspects of human maturity

108.   The Congregation for Catholic Education's *Basic Norms for the Formation of Permanent Deacons* highlights four aspects of human maturity that must be considered when developing formation programs for deacons. These include: (1) formation in the human virtues, (2) the capacity to relate to others, (3) affective maturity (including psychosexual maturity and health), and (4) training in freedom, which "includes the education of the moral conscience."[6] Deacons, above all, must be persons who can relate well to others.[7] This ability flows from an affective maturity that "presupposes . . . the victorious struggle against their own selfishness."[8] Mature ways of relating to others are important servant-leadership qualities. Those who aspire to this ministry need to collaborate well with others and to confront challenges in a constructive way. "A pre-condition for an authentic human maturity is training in freedom, which is expressed in obedience to the truth of one's own being."[9]

109.   Human formation aims to enhance the personality of the minister in such a way that he becomes "a bridge and not an obstacle for others in their meeting with Jesus Christ."[10] Accordingly, formation processes need to be structured so as to nurture and encourage the participants "to acquire and perfect a series of human qualities which will permit them to enjoy the trust of the community, to commit themselves with serenity to the pastoral ministry, to facilitate encounter and dialogue."[11] Therefore, all of these various aspects of human maturity must be carefully considered when planning the formation program and when assessing a participant's effective integration of them. If warranted, a participant may also consult (or be asked to do so) with a qualified professional, approved by the director of formation, to assist in this assessment.

Human formation aims to enhance the personality of the minister

Spiritual Dimension

110.   "Human formation leads to and finds its completion in the spiritual dimension of formation, which constitutes the heart and unifying center of every Christian formation. Its aim is to tend to the development of the new life received in Baptism."[12] Many directions lead to this goal, all of them fundamentally the work of the Holy Spirit. The spiritual life is, therefore, dynamic and never static. The first goal of spiritual formation is the establishment and nourishment of attitudes, habits, and practices that will set the foundation for a lifetime of ongoing spiritual discipline.

Spiritual foundations for discipleship and ministry

111.   A man should not be admitted to diaconal formation unless it is demonstrated that he is already living a life of mature Christian spirituality.[13] The spiritual dimension of formation should "affirm and strengthen" this spirituality, and it should emphasize "specific traits of diaconal spirituality."[14]

A mature spirituality in imitation of Jesus

112.   Configured sacramentally to Christ the Servant, a deacon's spirituality must be grounded in the attitudes of Christ. These include "simplicity of heart, total giving of self and disinterest for self, humble and helpful love for the brothers and sisters, especially the poorest, the suffering and the most needy, the choice of a lifestyle of sharing and poverty."[15] This diaconal spirituality is nourished by the Eucharist, which, "not by chance, characterizes the ministry of the deacon."[16] A diaconal spirituality is conditioned by participation in the apostolic ministry and should be marked by

openness to God's word, to the Church, and to the world.[17] The fundamental spiritual attitude should be one of openness to this word contained in revelation, as preached by the Church, celebrated in the liturgy and lived out in the lives of God's People. To herald the Gospel requires missionary zeal—a new evangelization—to bring God's love and salvation to all in word and action. The preaching of the word is always connected, therefore, with prayer, the celebration of the Eucharist, and the building of community. The earliest community of Christ's disciples was a model of this.[18] To attain an interior spiritual maturity requires an intense sacramental and prayer life.

OBJECTIVES

Goals of the spiritual dimension

113.   The objectives of the spiritual dimension in formation are (a) to deepen his prayer life—personal, familial, communal, and liturgical—with special emphasis upon participation in Eucharist, daily if possible; daily celebration of the Liturgy of the Hours, especially morning and evening prayer; *lectio divina*, devotion to the Blessed Virgin Mary and the saints; and regular reception of the Sacrament of Reconciliation; (b) to assist the participant, with the help of his spiritual director and those responsible for formation, to deepen and cultivate a service commitment to God's word, the Church, and the world; (c) to acquaint him with the Catholic spiritual tradition reflected in classic spiritual writings and in the lives of the saints, and with contemporary developments in spirituality—a faith seeking to be expressed and celebrated; (d) to affirm the Christian witness of matrimonial and celibate spirituality; (e) to incarnate his spirituality in the real life and history of the people whom he encounters each day in places where he lives, works, and serves.[19]

Discernment in spiritual formation

114.   Discernment is an essential spiritual process in determining the presence of a vocation to the diaconate, as well as the capacity to live it fully after ordination. The spiritual dimension of formation, therefore, should assist the participant in assessing the depth and quality of his integration of personal, family, employment, and ministerial responsibilities. Further, it should assist his growth in self-knowledge, in his commitment to Christ and his Church, and in his dedication to service, especially to the poor and those most suffering.[20] A strong spiritual life and a realistic commitment to serve people converge in the continual transformation of the participant's mind and heart in harmony with Christ.

115.   Spiritual formation helps the participant to develop the virtue of penance, which includes mortification, sacrifice, and generosity toward others. The participant must be open to conversion of heart about issues of justice, peace, and respect for life. He needs to be instructed on how his prayer, simplicity of life, and commitment to the poor add credibility to his capacity to witness and, as a deacon, to preach effectively the Word of God.[21]

Credibility in one's lifestyle

116.   Each person in formation is called to a mature relationship with those in authority that includes a spirit of trust, mutual respect, and obedience. Accountability in formation is an invitation to a deeper conversion. A spirit of service to others is finally an imitation of Christ himself, who came not to do his own will but the will of his Father.[22] Formation personnel, especially the spiritual director, should give instructions on the meaning of authentic obedience and help each participant to appreciate and practice it in his life.

Obedience and respect

117.   The role of the spiritual director, who must always be a priest,[23] is critical to the formation process, particularly in assisting the participant to discern and affirm the signs of his vocation.[24] An individual's spiritual director may be chosen directly by the participant with the approval of the bishop, or from a list of spiritual directors similarly approved. The distinction between internal and external forums must always be clearly maintained. A participant may also consult (or be requested to do so) with an advisor whom he may select with the approval of the director of formation. The advisor, however, does not substitute for the unique role of the spiritual director in formation and discernment.[25]

Spiritual director

Intellectual Dimension

118.   Intellectual formation offers the participant "substantial nourishment" for the pastoral, human, and spiritual dimensions of his life. Intellectual formation is a "precious instrument" for effective discernment and ministry. An increasingly educated society and the new roles of leadership in diaconal ministry require that a deacon be a knowledgeable and reliable witness to the faith and a spokesman for the Church's teaching. Therefore, the intellectual dimension of formation must be designed to communicate a knowledge of the faith and church tradition that is "complete and serious," so that each participant will be prepared to carry out his vital ministry.[26]

Knowledge of faith and Church

The commitment to study, which takes up no small part of the time of those preparing for the [diaconate], is not in fact an external and secondary dimension of their human, Christian, spiritual and vocational growth. In reality, through study, especially the study of theology, the future [deacon] assents to the Word of God, grows in his spiritual life and prepares himself to fulfill his pastoral ministry.[27]

OBJECTIVES

Goals of the intellectual dimension

119.   Deacons must first understand and practice the essentials of Christian doctrine and life before they can communicate them to others in a clear way in their ministries of word, liturgy, and charity. Sacred Scripture is the soul of the program. Around it are structured the other branches of theology. Liturgical studies are to be given prominence, as the participants are prepared to lead the faith community in prayer and sacramental life. Preaching, with its preparation and practice, requires a significant segment of time in the program of study. Attention should also be given to topics reflecting the specific needs of the Church in the United States: (1) a family life perspective; (2) respect for and understanding of our national multicultural diversity and the incorporation of the Gospel into all aspects of society; (3) the social dimension of the Gospel as taught by the Church, especially in the social encyclicals of the Popes, and the significant documents promulgated by the United States Conference of Catholic Bishops, with special reference to concerns surrounding immigration as experienced within the Church in America;[28] (4) the study of the beliefs and practices of other religions and Christian denominations—deepening a spirit of ecumenism and interreligious dialogue. Ample opportunities also need to be given to the study and practice of missiology—learning how to evangelize—so as to form deacons who will be actively present in society, offering true diaconal witness, entering into sincere dialogue with others, and cooperating in charity and justice to resolve common concerns.[29]

The intellectual content should be oriented toward a pastoral context

120.   The intellectual content should be organized, presented, and directed fundamentally to prepare participants for the pastoral context of service.[30] It should provide the participant with the knowledge, skills, and appreciation of the faith that he needs to effectively fulfill his ministry of word, liturgy, and charity. It should, therefore,

be authentic and complete. In spite of the diversity of subjects, the intellectual dimension should offer an overall vision of faith that brings unity and harmony to the educational process.[31] The theological formation of the participants needs to be presented as originating from within the Church's life of faith, worship, and pastoral care.[32] In this way, intellectual formation will be perceived as crucial to the deacon's responsible exercise of his ministry.

121.   The intellectual dimension should also be constructed to help the participant "to evaluate his society and culture in light of the Gospel and to understand the Gospel in the light of the particular features of the society and culture in which he will be serving."[33] Of equal importance is the discernment and understanding of what is shared in common, as well as the cultural and ethnic expressions of the faith.

Cultural analysis

122.   Since participants enter formation as mature men, the intellectual dimension of formation "should make use of the methods and processes of adult education. . . . [The participants] should be invited to draw and reflect upon their adult life and faith experiences."[34]

Adult educational methodology

123.   Theology is traditionally described as "faith seeking understanding." Therefore, the formation faculty and staff should structure an intellectual process that includes an invitation to each participant to reflect on his adult life and experience in the light of the Gospel and the Church's teaching. The intellectual dimension in each path in the formation program should be designed and presented in such a way as to integrate doctrine, morality, and spirituality.

Integration of learning and life

124.   The following criteria focus the preparation and presentation of a systematic, comprehensive, and integrated intellectual formation, faithful to the Magisterium of the Church. Based on Scripture and Tradition, the documents of the Second Vatican Council, the *Catechism of the Catholic Church*, and the *General Directory for Catechesis*,[35] this formation must take into account the following theological content:

Academic content

a.   Introduction to sacred Scripture and its authentic interpreta-
     tion; the theology of the Old and New Testaments; the interre-
     lation between Scripture, Tradition, and the Magisterium; the
     use of Scripture in spiritual formation, preaching, evangeliza-
     tion, catechesis, and pastoral activity in general

b.   Introduction to the study of the Fathers of the Church and an
     elementary knowledge of the history of the Church

c.   Fundamental theology, with illustration of the sources; topics
     and methods of theology; presentation of the questions relating
     to revelation and the formulation of the relationship between
     faith and reason, which will enable the participant to explain
     the reasonableness of the faith[36]

d.   Dogmatic theology, with its trinitarian, christological, pneuma-
     tological, and ecclesial dimensions, including the Church as a
     communion of churches—Latin and Eastern Catholic
     Churches;[37] Christian anthropology; sacraments; eschatology;
     Mariology

e.   Christian morality in its personal, familial, and social dimen-
     sions, including the social doctrine of the Church

f.   Spiritual theology, the spiritual traditions of the Church as
     applied to one's own spiritual journey, and the spiritual life of
     the faithful

g.   Liturgy and its historical, spiritual, and juridical aspects, with
     particular attention to the Rite of Christian Initiation of Adults
     and to the liturgical rites the deacon will celebrate

h.   Canon Law, especially canonical considerations of the rights
     and obligations of the clergy, and the canons applicable to
     Baptism, marriage, and Christian burial

i.   Ecumenism and interreligious dialogue principles, norms, and
     dimensions in pastoral ministry;[38]

j.   Theology of Catholic evangelization: "evangelization of cul-
     tures and the inculturation of the message of faith," multicul-
     tural expressions of the faith, and missiology[39]

125.   This content is structured further in Norms 5-12 at the end
of Chapter Six. Those responsible for the preparation of the academic component in the candidate and post-ordination paths of formation should determine a course of study that complies with this
content prior to ordination, as well as a course of study that will further develop this content after ordination as part of a structured

post-ordination program for continuing education and formation. Before ordination, the deacon candidate must demonstrate competence in all these areas.

Pastoral Dimension

126.   An integral formation must relate the human, spiritual, and intellectual dimensions to pastoral practice. "The whole formation imparted to [the participants] . . . aims at preparing them to enter into communion with the charity of Christ. . . . Hence their formation in its different aspects must have a fundamentally pastoral character."[40] Within that context, the pastoral dimension in formation is not merely an apprenticeship to familiarize the participant in diaconal formation with some pastoral techniques. Its aim, however, is to initiate the aspirant and candidate into the sensitivity of what it means to be a disciple of Jesus, who came to serve and not be served. Pastoral field education embodies this orientation, promoting learning through active engagement in a pastoral situation. Pastoral field education fosters a general integration in the formational process forging a close link between the human, spiritual, and intellectual dimensions in formation. Evangelization; Catholic schools; catechetics; religious education; youth ministry, social justice outreach opportunities; rural ministry; ecumenism; the care of the sick, elderly, and dying; as well as service opportunities in varied cultural settings indicate the breadth of experiences to which an aspirant and candidates may be exposed in the course of his pastoral field-education program.

Integrating role of pastoral formation

OBJECTIVES

127.   The pastoral dimension in diaconal formation should strengthen and enhance the exercise of the prophetic, priestly, and servant-leadership functions—deriving from his baptismal consecration—already lived and exercised by the participant in diaconal formation. In each path in formation, they must be taught how to proclaim the Christian message and teach it, how to lead others in communal celebrations of liturgical prayer, and how to witness to the Church in a Christian service marked by charity and justice. The demonstration of pastoral skills is a crucial element in the assessment of fitness for ordination. Therefore, the qualities to be developed for these tasks are as follows: a spirit of pastoral responsibility and servant-leadership; generosity and perseverance; creativity; respect for ecclesial communion; and filial obedience to the bishop.

Objectives of the pastoral dimension

Through his participation in pastoral field education, the participant should have a genuine confidence in his abilities and a realistic sense of his limitations.

Pastoral formation content

128.   Pastoral formation should take into account that those preparing for the diaconate have already been involved in the mission of the Church. The pastoral field education program should be designed, therefore, to build upon previous experiences and talents already displayed. In addition to identifying and developing the gifts already at work, the pastoral dimension of formation should aim at helping the participant to discover talents, perhaps unrecognized, and to develop the skills necessary for exercising the threefold diaconal ministry. A participant needs to demonstrate a genuine confidence in his own ability—a realistic sense of achieving the knowledge and skills required for an effective diaconal ministry—and a strong desire to serve in a broad range of ministerial circumstances.

Pastoral formation interfaces with spiritual formation

129.   Pastoral formation interfaces with spiritual formation. It is a formation for an ever-greater identification with the *diakonia* entrusted to the Church by Christ. Care is to be taken to introduce the participant actively into the pastoral life of the diocesan Church and to ensure periodic meetings with the diocesan bishop, priests, other deacons, religious, and laity serving in official ministry, to ensure a coordinated unity for different pastoral activities.[41] Supervised pastoral formation placements should be designed and adapted to the needs of the individual participant, helping him to gradually and appropriately experience in his pastoral placement what he has learned in his study.[42] He should also be given ample opportunities to share experiences with deacons already in ministry.

Pastoral theology

130.   Pastoral formation develops by means of a specific theological discipline and a practical internship. This theological discipline, traditionally called "pastoral theology," is "a scientific reflection on the Church as she is built up daily."[43] The pastoral dimension of formation needs to pay particular attention to the following elements.

a. **The Church's Ministry of the Word**—Proclamation of the word in the varied contexts of ministerial service: *kerygma*, catechesis, preparation for the sacraments, homiletics—both in theory and practice, evangelization and missiology

b. **The Church's Ministry of Liturgy**—Liturgical praxis: celebration of the sacraments and sacramentals, service at the altar

c. **The Church's Ministry of Charity and Justice**—Preaching, educating the Christian community on the social dimensions of the Gospel; fostering by facilitation, motivation, and organization the Church's ministry of charity and justice, and the preferential option for the poor.

The diakonia of word, liturgy, and charity

131.   As part of his pastoral field education formation, the candidate should acquire an appropriate multicultural awareness, exposure, and sensitivity, suitable to the needs of the diocese, including the possibility of learning a second language and studying its cultural context.

The life of the community, in particular the guidance of family teams, small communities, groups, and movements

132.

a. Certain technical subjects that prepare the participant for specific pastoral care can be useful, such as pastoral counseling, with particular emphasis on appropriate referral, especially as applied to family ministry; catechetical pedagogy; sacred music; ecclesiastical administration

b. A practical internship that permits the participant to encounter and respond in ministry to that which he has learned in his study

c. Progressive involvement in the pastoral activity of the diocese

d. The developing of the participant's commitment to ecumenism and interreligious dialogue; appropriate shared pastoral experiences should be considered[44]

e. A maturing in the participant of "a strong missionary sensitivity"[45]

f. According to particular situations and needs, an appropriate integration with other disciplines, such as philosophy, economics and politics, psychology, and sociology[46]

g. Information technology, distance learning, and the use of the Internet in pastoral ministry

Other recommended elements of the participant's pastoral formation

Theological reflection	133. Pastoral formation must include theological reflection so the participant may integrate his ministerial activity with the broad scope of diaconal studies. This process should lead him to a lifelong effort in reflecting on his ministry in the light of faith.

III. Additional Considerations

Topics of value in the United States	134. Attention should be given to the following topics which represent a value central to the life of the Catholic Church in the United States and, therefore, in the formation, ministry, and life of candidates and deacons.

A Family Life Perspective
INTRODUCTION

A family-centered formation	135. A family life perspective is rooted in the challenge of Pope John Paul II as stated in *Familiaris Consortio*: "No plan for organized pastoral work at any level must ever fail to take into consideration the pastoral area of the family."[47] Refocusing one's thinking from an individual-centered approach to a family-centered approach now represents an important component in organizing diaconal formation, ministry, and life.[48]
The family is the primary formation community	136. Individuals do not enter into formation alone. Those who participate in diaconal formation, married or unmarried, come with their families. They come as members of a family known as the "domestic Church" where life is shared and nurtured. They come from that primary community, where God is first discovered and known, into a new and wider community that can expand their love and deepen their faith. They come with their experiences of faith and personal life.
Family life requires a proper balance	137. Each participant must explore ways to keep his family life a priority in the face of the growing demands of formation and ministry, which include issues of age, faith, health, economics, employment, and relationships.

THE MARRIED PARTICIPANT

The role of the wife	138. In deciding to pursue a possible diaconal vocation, a married man must comply with the wishes of his wife, in a spirit of mutual commitment and love. A wife is an equal partner in the Sacrament

of Matrimony and is an individual person with her own gifts, talents, and call from God. A candidate's diaconal formation can be a unique and challenging situation and opportunity for his wife. She should be involved in the program in appropriate ways, remembering, however, that it is the husband who is responding to a call to the diaconate. The Church has determined that a married man cannot be considered for the diaconate without the consent of his wife.[49] After ordination, a deacon's wife needs to "be duly informed of [her] husband's activities in order to arrive at a harmonious balance between family, professional and ecclesial responsibilities."[50]

139.   The participation of a wife in her husband's formation program strengthens an awareness of the husband's diaconal vocation and helps the wife to accept the challenges and changes that will take place, should her husband be ordained. It also provides an opportunity for those responsible for diaconal formation to assess whether she has "the Christian moral character and attributes which will neither hinder [her] husband's ministry nor be out of keeping with it."[51] To help the candidate's wife to give an informed consent to her husband's request for ordination, it is necessary to include specific resources and programming addressed to her. When workshops and spiritual exercises for wives are planned, wives should be consulted to ascertain their questions and concerns. While every effort ought to be made to provide scheduling and material assistance to make wives' participation possible, care must simultaneously be taken to keep clear the essential distinction between ordained and familial life and the clear independence of diaconal ministry.[52]

Appropriate inclusion

140.   Children of participants also need to be included in the formation process in "appropriate ways."[53] This will depend, among other considerations, on their ages, circumstances, and interests. These occasions provide opportunities for parents and their children to support and assist each other in keeping communication open and expectations clear. Younger children and teens especially need to be encouraged to express their concerns about the public role of this ministry and how it affects their lives both within the family and among their peers. They need to express honestly their concerns over the commitment of time and energy by their parents and what this means to the life of the family and to each member. This is not only a family concern; it is a formation concern.

The role of children

Formation and family life	141. A man's diaconal formation can be a gift in the life of his family, providing it with an opportunity to explore together the meaning of discipleship, Church, and church vocations. It can strengthen the bonds between parents and their children through prayer, communication, and shared virtue. It can also be a powerful experience of community, service, and compassion.

THE UNMARRIED PARTICIPANT

Support and encourage his vocation	142. What has been described regarding the role of the family in the formation of a married man also applies to the family of the unmarried participant (i.e., one who never married, one now widowed, or one now divorced[54]). His family should likewise be invited to share appropriately in the formation community. His parents, siblings, children, and extended family need similar grounding in understanding the ministry of the deacon so they can be supportive and encouraging of his vocation.

143.   The unmarried participant must grow in clear and realistic understanding of the value of celibate chastity and its connection to diaconal ministry.[55] To be lived fruitfully, the value of celibacy must be internalized. To achieve these formation goals, the unmarried participant should be incorporated into a mentoring group composed of priests and celibate deacons from whom he can receive support and encouragement, a group where a dialogue on the challenges and a faith-filled response to a celibate lifestyle can be fostered.

Multicultural Diversity

Formation for ministry in a multicultural Church	144. Deacons are called to serve a multiracial, multiethnic, multicultural Church. Immigration will only increase the challenge. This changing face of the Catholic Church in the United States should have a significant effect on diaconal formation. The cultures and traditions of those in diaconal formation—mirroring as they do the rich diversity of gifts and unity in faith—need to be respected, valued, and understood. Formation must be sensitive and responsive to the circumstances of different cultures,[56] especially in their unique patterns of learning and expressing their understanding. There should be formal instruction regarding the developmental role and function of culture in the life of the individual and community. Recognizing the cultural diversity of the Catholic Church in the United States and incorporating experiences and an appreciation

of it enhances the present and future ministerial effectiveness of each participant.

145.   Formation objectives and methods should accommodate an appropriate inculturation of each participant for his effective service within a multicultural community. Given the ethnic and racial diversity of our national population and the mobility that is so characteristic of our society, a participant in diaconal formation ought to have meaningful cross-cultural experiences and specific training for ministry in his own cultural context. This would include reasonable levels of language study in areas where large numbers of Catholics are not proficient in English. As an ordained servant-leader in a Church called to welcome and embrace all people, the deacon should be a living example of that spirit, particularly conscious of the potential for misunderstanding and alienation that can occur when cultural, ethnic, or racial diversity occasions discrimination rather than social harmony.[57]

Appropriate inculturation of each participant

Practical Aspects of Charity

146.   The social encyclicals of the Popes, and the significant documents promulgated by the United States Conference of Catholic Bishops on the integrity of human life from conception to death, on the economy, on racism, on immigration, on peace have focused attention on the social dimension of the Gospel. In a world that seeks to privatize religious commitment, diaconal formation should appropriately emphasize the social dimension of the Gospel, its concern for human life, for justice in the marketplace, and for peace in the world. A major resource in meeting this essential challenge is the *Guidelines for the Study and Teaching of the Church's Social Doctrine in the Formation of Priests,* from the Congregation for Catholic Education.

Social dimension of the Gospel

147.   The ministry of charity is "most characteristic of the deacon."[58] "In fact, with sacred ordination, [the deacon] is constituted a living icon of Christ the servant within the Church."[59] Therefore, as he conforms his life to Christ the Servant, making himself a generous and faithful servant of God and of those in need, especially among the poorest and those most suffering,[60] he helps to shape the vitality and genuineness of the exercise of the corporal and spiritual works of charity in the life of the believing community. His

Deacon: A living icon of Jesus, the servant

attentiveness to the manifold physical, emotional, social, and spiritual needs of people in his immediate environment and throughout the world reminds the Church that it is a servant-people sent into a needy world.[61] Within this commitment to a strong social consciousness, an essential emphasis emerges: "The practice and the commandment of love and mercy in everything which, in the spirit of the Gospel, gives priority to the poor."[62]

The spirit of the Gospel

148.   From its beginnings, the ministry of the deacon encompassed stewardship of the Church's material goods, making evident the claim of the poor on the resources of the community. Deacons helped to ensure that the allocation of those resources made provision for meaningful assistance to those who suffered from poverty, hunger, homelessness, and disease. Today, the restored diaconate maintains this traditional stewardship through its commitment to the poor. The deacon's service encompasses a witness to charity that may assume different forms, depending on what responsibilities the bishop assigns to the deacon.[63]

Catholic social teaching

149.   Although all those in sacred orders have a responsibility to preach justice, the deacon may have a particular advantage in bringing this message to the laity because he lives and works in the secular world. The deacon, because of his familiarity with the day-to-day realities and rhythms of the family, neighborhood, and workplace, can relate the rich tradition of Catholic social teaching to the practical problems experienced by people. He also may serve to link the Catholic Church to other Christian communities, other faith traditions, and civic organizations to address pressing social needs and to foster a collaborative sharing of material resources and personnel in response to those needs.[64]

150.   The deacon, as a servant of the Church's ministry of charity and justice, helps the faith community to understand and carry out its baptismal responsibilities. Formation programs, therefore, can help the participant to grow in an understanding of the Church's teaching and tradition of social justice. They also can impart the skills needed for promoting that teaching in the marketplace, parish, and diocese. Formation programming needs to provide opportunities to include an ever-deepening reflection upon the participant's experience and his growing commitment to the Church's social teaching.[65]

A Spirit of Ecumenism and Interreligious Dialogue

151.   The Second Vatican Council taught that the restoration of full visible communion among all Christians is the will of Christ and essential to the life of the Catholic Church.[66] An ecumenical spirit should be integrated into all aspects of formation. Those who are or will be engaged in pastoral ministry must acquire "an authentically ecumenical disposition"[67] in their lives and ministry. The purpose of formation in ecumenism is to educate hearts and minds in the necessary human and religious dispositions that will favor the search for Christian unity. A genuine ecumenism should be thoroughly incorporated into all aspects of diaconal formation,[68] remembering that "genuine ecumenical formation must not remain solely academic; it should also include ecumenical experience."[69]

Ecumenism and dialogue

152.   The Second Vatican Council also urged "its sons and daughters to enter with prudence and charity into discussion and collaboration with members of other religions."[70] Such a spirit must imbue a desire for ecumenical and interreligious cooperation with Jews, Muslims, and members of other religions. The formation program must assist the participant in achieving a spirit of welcome, respect, and collaboration among people of good will. "The concerns of justice, peace, and the integrity of human life join together all churches and all religions."[71] Diaconal formation should model and facilitate this collaborative cooperation.

Interreligious cooperation

IV. Assessment: Integrating the Four Dimensions in Formation Programming

153.   "To each individual the manifestation of the Spirit is given for some benefit."[72] All ministry flows out of the gifts of the Holy Spirit. These gifts are given to the People of God not for the benefit of the individual minister but for the benefit of the Church. As a result, any discernment of gifts and charisms must involve the ecclesial community. Since the charisms are ecclesial, any discernment process must also be ecclesial in nature. This is especially true for the ordained ministries of the Church. An individual who presents himself for ordination to the diaconate is accountable to the Church, who mediates—confirms—his vocation.

Discernment must be ecclesial in nature

154.   It is essential, therefore, that those who are responsible for selection and formation, including pastoral placement, discern whether the participant has integrated the various dimensions in formation that are needed for an effective diaconal ministry. Further, consultation with the participant's pastor, the faculty, other pastoral field education supervisors, mentors, those whom the participant serves, and, if married, his wife is crucial to the discernment process. The surest indicator, however, is the participant's previous and present effectiveness in Church service.

155.   If conducted seriously and communicated frankly, assessments can be valuable occasions for the discernment, affirmation, and development of a vocation. Assessments should be made and communicated on a regular basis. There are multiple ways of assessing, including self-assessment, faculty and mentor assessment, and peer and pastoral supervisory assessment, to name but a few. Different situations will require different forms and levels of assessment.

156.   Every assessment, however, has a dual purpose. It affirms the participant in identifying his gifts and capabilities, exhibits areas for his further growth and development, and indicates his limitations. It concurrently provides a similar assessment of the formation program itself. The assessment outcome of an individual participant can demonstrate the program's achievement in integrating the various dimensions of formation, that is, the effectiveness of its structures and scheduling, and the competency of its faculty, staff, and administrators. Simply stated, the assessment of the individual participant also points out the strength, potential, and limitation of the formation program.

157.   The following are some indicators that a formation program is successful, measured by the participant's ability to manifest

1. An increase in holiness of life
2. An ability to clearly articulate the Catholic faith
3. The capacity to apply church teaching and practice to concrete societal issues and pastoral concerns
4. A sensitivity to inculturate the Gospel within the communities in which he lives, works, and ministers

5. His embrace of the universal nature of the Church and its missionary-evangelical spirit
6. A balanced capacity for and commitment to the ministries of word, liturgy, and charity, demonstrated in his words and deeds
7. A commitment to ongoing growth in the human, spiritual, intellectual, and pastoral dimensions of formation
8. A capacity to foster the communion and mission of the lay faithful, in collaboration with the bishop and diocesan priests
9. An obedient and humble service to all in the name of the Church
10. His ability to celebrate, in accordance with the Church's legislation and with due reverence and devotion, those liturgical and sacramental acts that the Church entrusts to the deacon.

158.   A well-conceived diocesan formation program will comply fully with the Congregation for Catholic Education's document *Basic Norms for the Formation of Permanent Deacons*, as well as this *Directory.*

NORMS

1. There are three separate but integral paths that constitute a unified diocesan formation program for deacons: aspirant, candidate and post-ordination. (104)
2. Each path should include the four dimensions for a complete formation process: human, spiritual, intellectual, and pastoral. (104)
3. The role of the spiritual director, who must always be a priest, is critical to the formation process, particularly in assisting the participant in discerning and affirming the signs of his vocation. (117)
4. Intellectual formation must introduce the diaconal candidate and the ordained deacon to the fundamental teachings of the Church covering the areas delineated by the document *Basic Norms for the Formation of Permanent Deacons*, as well as in this *Directory.* It is essential that before ordination the candidate have a thorough knowledge of the Catholic faith and be able to communicate it effectively. (124)
5. During formation, the aspirant and candidate should have ample opportunities to participate appropriately in pastoral experience. (128-132)

6. Pastoral formation must include theological reflection so the participant may integrate his ministerial activity with the broad scope of diaconal studies. (133)
7. A married man cannot be considered for the diaconate without the consent of his wife. (138)
8. While every effort ought to be made to involve the wife of a married candidate and deacon in an appropriate level of participation in her husband's formation, care must simultaneously be taken to keep clear the essential distinction between ordained and familial life and the clear independence of diaconal ministry. (139)
9. The cultures and traditions of those in diaconal formation—mirroring as they do the rich diversity of gifts in the Church—need to be respected and valued. Formation, therefore, must be sensitive and adapted to the circumstances of different cultures. (144)
10. Assessments are valuable occasions for the discernment, affirmation, and development of a participant's vocation. Assessments should be made and communicated on a regular basis. (155)
11. A well conceived diocesan formation program will comply fully with the document of the Congregation for Catholic Education *Basic Norms for the Formation of Permanent Deacons,* as well as this *Directory.* (158)

NOTES

1   PDV, no. 42.

2   BNFPD, nos. 66-88.

3   PDV, no. 43.

4   Congregation for the Clergy, *General Directory for Catechesis* (GDC) (August 15, 1997) (Washington, D.C.: United States Catholic Conference-Libreria Editrice Vaticana, 1998), nos. 222-223.

5   Congregation for the Evangelization of Peoples, *Guide for Catechists* (December 3, 1993) (Washington, D.C.: United States Catholic Conference, 1993), no. 21.

6   BNFPD, no. 66-70.

7   Ibid., no. 67.

8   Ibid., no. 68.

9   Ibid., no. 69; cf. PDV, no. 44.

10   Ibid., no. 66, citing PDV, no. 43.

11   Ibid., no. 66.

12   Ibid., no. 71.

13   Ibid., nos. 32-33.

14   Ibid., no. 71.

15   Ibid., no. 72.

16   Ibid., no. 73.

17   PDV, nos. 47-49.

18   Cf. Acts 2-4; 1:14.

19   DMLPD, nos. 50-62; cf. BNFPD, no. 12.

20   BNFPD, no. 11.

21   Ibid., no. 72; cf. PDV, no. 30.

22   Jn 5:30.

23   BNFPD, no. 23.

24   Ibid.

25   Ibid., nos. 70, 76; cf. PDV, no. 66.

26   Ibid., no. 79.

27   PDV, no. 51.

28   Pope John Paul II, Post-Synodal Exhortation, *The Church in America* (*Ecclesia in America*) (Washington, D.C.: United States Catholic Conference, 1999).

29   PDV, nos. 51-56.

30   Ibid., no. 57.

31   BNFPD, no. 85.

32   PDV, no. 53.

33   PDG (1984), no. 76.

34   Ibid., no. 77.

35   GDC, no. 120.

36   Cf. Pope John Paul II, Encyclical Letter, *On the Relationship Between Faith and Reason* (*Fides et Ratio*) (Washington, D.C.: United States Catholic Conference, 1998).

37   Committee on the Relationship between Eastern and Latin Catholic Church, National Conference of Catholic Bishops, *Eastern Catholics in the United States of America* (Washington, D.C.: United States Catholic Conference, 1999).

38   Pontifical Council for Promoting Christian Unity, *The Ecumenical Dimension in the Formation of Pastoral Workers* (March 9, 1998), in *Ecumenical Formation of Pastoral Workers* (Washington, D.C.: United States Catholic Conference, 1998); cf. BNFPD, no. 88.

39   PDV, no. 55.

40   Ibid., no. 57; cf. BNFPD, no. 85.

41   DMLPD, no. 78.

42   BNFPD, no. 87.

43   PDV, no. 57.

44   Pontifical Council for Promoting Christian Unity, op. cit.

45   BNFPD, no. 88.

46   Ibid., nos. 81, 86.

47   Pope John Paul II, Apostolic Exhortation, *On the Family* (*Familiaris Consortio*) (Washington, D.C.: United States Catholic Conference, 1981). no. 70.

48   Aspirants, candidates and deacons will be required to participate in classes, pastoral ministries and services, and spiritual exercises. It is necessary, therefore, to focus this injunction proposed by the Holy Father in his encyclical letter, *Familiaris Consortio*, in its application to the specific pastoral work of organizing the formation, ministry, and life of aspirants, candidates and deacons—"No plan for organized pastoral work at any level must ever fail to take into consideration the pastoral area of the family." To assist the director of formation and the director of deacon personnel to comply with this injunction in preparing and implementing a diocesan plan, organization, and schedule for the formation, ministry and life of aspirants, candidates, and deacons, *A Family Perspective in Church and Society*, published by the United States Conference of Catholic Bishops' Committee on Marriage and Family (Tenth Anniversary Edition, September, 1998) will prove useful. In reflecting upon the experience of the Synod of Bishops convoked in 1980 by John Paul II on the topic of family life in the modern world, as well as his apostolic exhortation in 1981 on the family, the committee authored this document with the intent "to elicit continuing pastoral action in support of family life" (p. v). The entire document needs to be read, studied, and reflected upon "so that the concept of a family perspective will have practical implications"(p. vi) in the formation, ministry, and life of aspirants, candidates, and deacons. It will be helpful in the scheduling of formation events to include the formation participants. Therefore, "to develop a family perspective in policies, programs, ministries, and services," those responsible for formation need to:

- Keep up-to-date with family changes and trends in the nation and in their locale, and then examine their policies, programs, ministries, and service in light of this information.
- Be sensitive to the fact that many kinds of families participate in programs.
- Be sensitive to the special needs families experience and the pressures and stress these needs create. Leaders need to help families identify these pressures and [in partnership help families] deal with them.
- Be sensitive, in planning, to the time and energy commitments of families where both parents—or the only parent—are employed.
- Be sensitive to the economic pressures families experience today.
- Understand that all programs affect families, even programs aimed at individuals. All social institutions, including the Church, make a direct or indirect impact on the unity, well-being, health, and stability of families. There is a tendency to replace family responsibilities, in part or in their entirety, by social institutions or to marginalize families' participation in the various programs and services provided by these institutions because these services are designed primarily for individuals.
- Help families manage their coordinating and mediating responsibility, rather than complicate it. For example, parish leaders often tell family members that their participation in parish programs is imperative. But families need to be active participants in determining parish priorities, and they have a responsibility to determine their participation . . . based on a realistic assessment of their energy, family time, and resources.
- What the Church does and how it does it affect the unity, well-being, health, and stability of families. Church leaders need to be more aware of how the Church's policies, programs, ministries, and services can either help or hinder families in fulfilling their own basic responsibilities. Church leaders need to see themselves as partners with families.

FP, pp. 10-11, 46-47 (Cf., also, DMLPD, no. 61; BNFPD, no. 27).

49   CIC, c. 1031: 2; cf. BNFPD, no. 37.

50   DMLPD, no. 61.

51   BNFPD, no. 37.

52   DMLPD, no. 81.

53   BNFPD, no. 56; cf. DMLPD, nos. 61, 81.

54   "While the decision to accept such a [divorced] man remains with the bishop, it must be exercised with the highest caution and prudence. This is particularly so if the candidate has had his marriage declared null by a Church tribunal on psychological grounds (cf. Letter of the Sacred Congregation for Catholic Education, dated 8 July 1983, Prot. N. 657/83 & 982/80/136, to His Excellency the Most Rev. John Roach, Archbishop of St. Paul and Minneapolis, President of the Episcopal Conference of the USA, concerning the admission to seminary of men whose marriages have been declared null by ecclesiastical tribunals)."

Congregation for Catholic Education and the Congregation for the Clergy, *Joint Study of the US Draft Document—National Directory for the Formation, Ministry and Life of Permanent Deacons in the United States*, Prot. No. 78/2000 (March 4, 2002).

55   PDV, no. 29.

56   BNFPD, no. 10.

57   Bishops' Committee on Migration, National Conference of Catholic Bishops, *One Family Under God, Revised Edition* (Washington, D.C.: United States Catholic Conference, 1998), p. 20.

58   BNFPD, no. 9.

59   Ibid., no. 11.

60   DMLPD, no. 38.

61   PDV, nos. 10, 27, 32; Second Vatican Council, *Decree on the Missionary Activity of the Church (Ad Gentes Divinitus)* (December 7, 1965) (Washington, D.C.: United States Catholic Conference, 1965), nos. 11-12.

62   Congregation for Catholic Education, *Guidelines for the Study and Teaching of the Church's Social Doctrine in the Formation of Priests* (Washington, D.C.: United States Catholic Conference, 1988), no. 61.

63   DMLPD, nos. 37-38, 42.

64   Pontifical Council for Promoting Christian Unity, *The Ecumenical Dimension in the Formation of Pastoral Workers*, op. cit.; cf. Pontifical Council for Promoting Christian Unity, *Ecumenical Formation: Ecumenical Reflections and Suggestions* (May 20, 1993), III, nos. 17-25, in *Ecumenical Formation of Pastoral Workers* (Washington, D.C.: United States Catholic Conference, 1998).

65   Committee on Domestic Social Policy and Committee on International Policy, National Conference of Catholic Bishops, *Communities of Salt and Light: Reflections on the Social Mission of the Parish* (Washington, D.C.: United States Catholic Conference, 1994).

66   Cf. Second Vatican Council, *Decree on Ecumenism (Unitatis Redintegratio)* (November 21, 1964) (Washington, D.C.: United States Catholic Conference, 1964), nos. 1-4.

67   Pontifical Council for Promoting Christian Unity, *Directory for the Application of Principles and Norms on Ecumenism* (March 25, 1993), no. 70.

68   Pontifical Council for Promoting Christian Unity, *The Ecumenical Dimension in the Formation of Pastoral Workers*, op. cit., nos. 2-4; cf. nos. 16-29.

69   Ibid., no. 28.

70   Second Vatican Council, *Declaration on the Relation of the Church to Non-Christian Religions (Nostra Aetate)* (October 28, 1965) (Washington, D.C.: United States Catholic Conference, 1965), no. 2.

71   National Conference of Catholic Bishops, *Program of Priestly Formation, Fourth Edition* (Washington, D.C.: United States Catholic Conference, 1993), no. 21.

72   1 Cor 12:7.

CHAPTER FOUR

VOCATION, DISCERNMENT, AND SELECTION

I. Promotion and Recruitment

159.   The First Letter of St. Paul to Timothy provides the first principle for the selection of deacons: "They should be tested first; then, if there is nothing against them, let them serve as deacons."[1] St. Thomas Aquinas offers an additional insight: Grace builds on nature. Those who have worked closely with the reestablishment of the diaconate conclude that the diaconate is a particular vocation called forth by the Holy Spirit, that a successful process of training and development can only cooperate with fundamental preexisting traits and dispositions that point to a diaconal vocation and build upon them, and that the process of training and development can be successful only in supportive life circumstances.

Grace builds on nature

160.   The promotion and recruitment of qualified men for the diaconate should be a collaborative ministry between the staffs of the diocesan vocations office and the diaconate office, as well as the diocesan bishop and pastors. If the diocesan Church wishes to nominate appropriate men, it may be helpful for the diocesan diaconate office to prepare guidelines, approved by the bishop, that provide specific information about recruitment, as well as the selection and formation processes. If the reestablishment of the diaconate is made part of a coherent diocesan pastoral plan for ministry in which deacons will have an important role, then the diocese and parishes can more easily identify and recruit potential candidates, describe to them the challenges and opportunities of diaconal ministry in the diocese, and urge them to consider it as a service to which they can commit themselves.

161.   The Church in the United States is enriched by the diversity of its cultural, racial, and ethnic communities. Since these communities share in the responsibility for promoting Church vocations, their leaders ought to be formally invited and included in the planning and implementation of vocation programs directed to their

Cultural, racial, and ethnic involvement in promoting church vocations

communities. Their support and encouragement will effectively assist in the recruitment of qualified nominees from their communities. Representatives of U.S. ethnic and cultural communities—such as Americans of African, Pacific Asian, Native American, and Hispanic heritage—who participate as consultants to the diaconate office, can provide significant insight on cultural subtleties and their effect upon discernment and formation programming, including pastoral placement.

Hispanic Americans

162.   Of particular importance in the United States is the large Hispanic Catholic population. Knowledge of Spanish and of Hispanic cultures is important in both recruiting and retaining Hispanic candidates. In each path in formation, essential resources— e.g., translators, textbooks, mentors, community support—should be provided to ensure the inclusion of each participant.

Study of language and culture

163.   Care ought to be taken, especially in the post-ordination path in formation, to provide opportunities for English-speaking deacons to learn Spanish, or other appropriate languages used in the diocese, on a conversational level. The opportunity for formal study of Hispanic and other cultures also should be provided. Further, the study of English and the historical development of a multicultural society within the United States should be provided to those whose primary language is not English.

Multicultural sensitivity

164.   The above discussion regarding the recruitment and retention of Hispanic candidates applies to each cultural, racial, and ethnic community. Those responsible for recruitment, discernment, and formation have a responsibility to exercise multicultural sensitivity. They need to appreciate cultural subtleties and differences, acknowledging the historical constrictions experienced within these communities. Further, familiarity with family structures and traditions is important. This cultural/racial/ethnic orientation and sensitivity enables recruiters and those involved in formation to competently discern and foster diaconal vocations within these diverse faith communities.

II. The Mystery of Vocation

165.   "The history . . . of every Christian vocation, is the history of an *inexpressible dialogue between God and human beings*, between the love of God who calls and the freedom of individuals who respond lovingly to him."[2] This calling-forth from God is marked first in the reception of the sacraments of Christian initiation. From out of this body of believers Christ then calls some of his disciples, and the Church, discerning their vocational charism, asks the bishop to ordain them to a service of the whole Church.

Personal and public call

166.   From the experience of the restored diaconate in the United States, certain behavioral patterns have been discerned among exemplary deacons: a "natural inclination of service to the . . . Christian community,"[3] and to all in need; psychological integrity; a capacity for dialogue, which implies a sense of docility and openness; the ability to share one's faith yet listen respectfully to other points of view; the capacity to listen carefully and without prejudices—respecting people in the context of their religion, race, gender, ethnicity, and culture; good communication skills; a sense of responsibility that includes the fulfilling of one's word and completing one's work; self-directed and collaborative accountability; balanced and prudent judgment; generosity in service; and the ability to lead, motivate, facilitate, and animate others into appropriate action and service.[4]

Diaconal call

Balance

167.   The profile is completed with certain spiritual and evangelical qualities. Among these are a sound faith; good Christian reputation; active involvement in the Church's apostolate; personal integrity, maturity, and holiness; regular participation in the Church's sacramental life; evidence of recognized, ongoing commitment to the Church's life and service; participation in faith enrichment opportunities (e.g., retreats, days of recollection, adult education programming); a positive and stable marriage, if married, or a mature celibate state of life, if single; active membership in a Christian community; capacity for obedience and fraternal communion; and a deep spirituality and prayer life. The presence of these qualities, experienced in kindness and humility, may demonstrate a call to the Order of Deacons.[5]

faith in action

Element of readiness

168.   Additional considerations that need to be stressed are the element of readiness and the timeliness of one's response to a vocation. Since inquirers to the diaconate have many commitments to family, career, employment, community, and church service, it is a matter of prudential judgment to explore not only whether the call to the diaconate is from the Holy Spirit, but also whether the inquirer is ready and able to respond to that call at the present time.

III. The Discernment of the Call

Personal discernment

169.   The first stirrings of a vocation to the diaconate are often explored at a personal level and usually begin with seeking information about the diaconate and formation. Here, an individual initially reflects upon the nature of his perceived call. Primacy must be given at this time to the spiritual dimension, and central to this is spiritual guidance. "Because every spiritual journey is personal and individual, it requires personal guidance."[6] The pastor and others on the parish staff are particular resources at this time.

Family discernment

170.   As the majority of those who inquire about the diaconate are married, they should be directed to pay particular attention to discussing their possible vocation with their wives and families. The initial information and conversations with their pastor and others should assist and encourage these discussions. For a married man, the support and consent of his wife is required. Therefore, both spouses need to make sure that support and consent, even at this early stage of discernment, arise from an informed understanding. Many regions and cultures also place emphasis on the participation of the extended family. This, too, is an important resource for discernment.

Communal discernment

171.   An inquiry and eventual application for entrance into diaconal formation is not just a personal and family journey. The Church must accompany it. The parish is the primary experience of Church for most inquirers. It is the responsibility of this community and, in particular, its pastor to invite from among its members those who may be qualified to serve as ordained ministers of the Church.[7] Similarly, those church and community agencies that have often carried out the Church's mission of charity and justice have a unique opportunity to call forth appropriate nominees from among their personnel.

172.   An inquiry about the diaconate and the formation process eventually includes the diocesan Church. Information sessions, the exploration of the criteria for a diaconal vocation, and particular counsel presented by the diocesan diaconate office can aid an individual in his decision to move forward to a formal application.

Ecclesial discernment

173.   When the inquirer is presented by his pastor and submits an application, the formal process for admission begins. This initial discernment is continued with particular focus on the applicant's abilities and potential for ordained ministry. Both the applicant and the diocesan Church enter into an intensive screening process.

Careful scrutiny

IV. Admission and Selection Procedures

The Role of the Pastor and Parish Community

174.   The inquirer who seeks consideration for ordination to the diaconate needs to enter into dialogue with his parish community. It is the pastor who initially presents him for consideration into diaconal formation through a letter that confirms he is a practicing Catholic of good repute and in good standing.[8]

Community recommendation

The Role of the Diocese

175.   The director of formation, who coordinates the selection process, arranges an interview with the diocese's committee on admission and scrutinies.[9] The purpose of the interview is to assess the applicant's level of awareness of a diaconal vocation, as well as to obtain information and background on his family life, employment stability, and general aptitude for diaconal ministry. The interview must include his wife, if he is married, and any children living at home.

Admission interview

176.   As part of the application process, those charged with admission must—with appropriate care for confidentiality and manifestation of conscience—explore for the presence of impediments to ordination.[10] If canonical dispensations are required, these must be obtained before admission to aspirant formation.

Impediments to ordination

177.   Appropriate psychological consultation may be included as part of the application process, but always with the written consent of the applicant.[11] Those selected as psychological consultants must

Psychological consultation

use psychological methods in harmony with Christian anthropology and Catholic teaching, particularly with respect to the theology of the diaconal vocation, the various states of life of the deacon, and the basic human qualities expected of a mature deacon. They also should obtain any pertinent and helpful information received in the admission process regarding the applicant. Care also must be taken in the selection of psychological consultants who will be assigned to applicants whose primary language is not English.

Required Application Documents

Required forms | 178.   Required application documents include the following:

a.   A church certificate of Baptism, Confirmation, and, if relevant, marriage, issued within the past six months[12]

b.   Proof of age: In accord with Canon Law,[13] the United States Conference of Catholic Bishops has established the minimum age of ordination at thirty-five years

c.   A completed application form, and, as appropriate, a consent form regarding psychological consultation and the confidentiality of consultative reports[14]

d.   A recent photograph of the nominee[15] and, if married, of his wife, for administrative and faculty identification

e.   A personal handwritten statement from the wife of a married applicant indicating her initial consent for his application and entrance into aspirant formation[16]

f.   Letters of recommendation[17]

g.   A recent medical certificate[18]

h.   An official transcript of past or present academic studies, if applicable[19]

i.   "A written report of the rector of any previous house in which the candidate has spent time in formation,"[20] including "explicit reference to the evaluations of the candidate and the votes he received"[21]

j.   A background check of each nominee under the auspices of the diocesan diaconate office

k.   Proof of legal residency in the diocese[22]

l.   A letter of recommendation from the applicant's employer[23]

Discernment of Readiness for the Aspirant Path in Formation

179.   Assessment of readiness at the application level is accomplished in a variety of ways. Common resources are letters of recommendation by those who know the applicant; a self-assessment prepared by the applicant, usually as an autobiographical statement; an interview with the committee on admission and scrutinies; and a review of his pastoral experience, especially noting any experience with the poor and the marginalized. Intellectual readiness is often assessed on the basis of prior experience through academic transcripts from schools attended and through evidence of participation in a lay ecclesial ministry formation program, parish adult education programs, or similar adult religious training.

Assessment of readiness

V. Admission into the Aspirant Path in Formation

180.   The diocese's committee on admission and scrutinies should develop a procedural process to review the application dossier of each applicant. Since admission into formation occurs through two distinct but unified processes—(1) acceptance into the aspirant path; (2) admittance into the candidate path in diaconal formation[24]—the committee should nominate to the bishop only those applicants whom they have judged as possessing the necessary qualities for entrance and successful completion of the aspirant path. Upon reviewing the recommendation, vote, and rationale of the committee, the bishop is the one who decides whether to admit the applicant into the aspirant path. If an applicant is judged not to be ready but to be a suitable aspirant in the future, the director of formation should convey to the applicant various options for how he might prepare himself to achieve the basic entrance requirements. It is also essential for the director of formation to keep frequent contact with these potential candidates.

Committee on admission and scrutinies

181.   With the acceptance of the applicant into aspirant formation, the admission process continues with an assessment of readiness for entrance into the candidate path in formation. This phase of discernment extends throughout the entire aspirant formation process, thereby allowing ample opportunity for personal observations, dialogue, interviews, and additional assessments of each aspirant.

NORMS

1. The inquirer who seeks consideration for ordination to the permanent diaconate needs to enter into dialogue with his parish since it is the pastor who is required to initially present him for diaconal formation. (174)
2. A formal application process, as well as a committee on admission and scrutinies, should be in place to review and nominate applicants. (175, 284)
3. As part of the application process, those charged with admission must—with appropriate care for confidentiality and manifestation of conscience—explore for the presence of canonical impediments to ordination. If canonical dispensations are required, these must be obtained before admission to aspirant formation. (176)
4. Required application documents are listed in paragraph 178.
5. With acceptance into aspirant formation, the admission process continues with an assessment of readiness for entrance into the candidate path in formation. (181)

NOTES

1   1 Tm 3:10.

2   BNFPD, no. 29, citing PDV, no. 36.

3   DMLPD, no. 49, citing Pope Paul VI, Apostolic Letter, *Sacrum Diaconatus Ordinem* (June 18, 1967), no. 8.

4   BNFPD, no. 32.

5   Ibid., nos. 31-33.

6   National Conference of Catholic Bishops, *Program for Priestly Formation, Fourth Edition* (Washington, D.C.: United States Catholic Conference, 1993), no. 280.

7   BNFPD, no. 40.

8   Ibid. This letter should attest that the man shows evidence of the qualities, attitudes, experience, and spirituality deemed necessary for admission into formation, namely, that he is

    a)   Actively involved in parish and other community service

    b)   In full communion with the Church (At least two or three years should elapse between a convert's or returning Catholic's entry into the Church and his acceptance into formation; care must be given to someone in whom a sudden conversion experience seems to precipitate a diaconal vocation.)

    c)   In a positive and stable marriage, if married, or in a mature celibate state of life, if single

    d)   If married, has the consent of his wife (An applicant whose marriage has been annulled should be screened carefully to ascertain if and how previous obstacles to a marriage commitment might affect his viability as a candidate for the diaconate. Care also should be extended to those who are recently widowed—normally, at least two years should elapse *prior* to acceptance; those recently married should live their married vocation for three years prior to requesting admittance.)

    e)   Properly motivated and gives evidence of an overall personal balance and moral character

    f)   A frequent participant in adult faith enrichment opportunities (e.g., retreats, days of reflection, spiritual direction, study of Scripture and church teachings)

    g)   Free of canonical impediments or irregularities (CIC, cc. 1040-1042)

9   Cf. this *Directory*, Chapter Eight, no. 284, on committee on admission and scrutinies.

10   BNFPD, no. 35; cf. Footnote 39 of BNFPD, no. 35.

11   Ibid., no. 70.

12   If the information regarding Confirmation or marriage, if relevant, is not recorded on the baptismal record, separate certificates for Confirmation and marriage are to be obtained (cf. CIC, cc. 1033; 1050:3; 241:2); annulment documents should also be obtained, if applicable.

13   CIC, c. 1031:3.

14   The application form should provide information on his family, as well as his religious, academic, employment, and service history, and a personal handwritten statement requesting admission into aspirant formation, indicating his motivation for seeking ordination to the

diaconate, his willingness to pledge his service to the diocesan Church, *and* his ability to fulfill the requirements of aspirant formation, if accepted (cf. CL, Enclosure I, 9; Enclosure II, 1): "It is necessary that this request be composed by the candidate personally and written out in his own hand and may not be a copied formulary, or worse, a photocopied text (cf. CIC, c. 1034:1)." (CL, Enclosure II, 1)

15   CL, Enclosure I, 5.

16   Cf. Note 14 above. This letter also should indicate her willingness to participate in the formation program as required.

17   CL, Enclosures I, 11. Letters should be requested from priests, deacons, parishioners, and colleagues.

18   Ibid., 7.

19   Ibid., 3 and 4.

20   Ibid., 10.

21   Ibid., 4; cf. CL, 8.

22   Cf. CIC, c. 265.

23   The contact with the employer provides a way to inform him of the applicant's possible participation in a program of education that may require occasional time alterations in his work schedule.

24   BNFPD, nos. 40, 45.

CHAPTER FIVE

ASPIRANT PATH IN DIACONAL FORMATION

I. Introduction

182.   Upon completion of the initial inquiry process, the bishop may accept some inquirers into aspirancy. This aspirant path in diaconal formation, as described in this *Directory,* corresponds to the "propaedeutic period" required by the *Basic Norms for the Formation of Permanent Deacons* of the Congregation for Catholic Education.[1] The aspirant path is primarily a time to discern the capability and readiness of an aspirant to be nominated to the bishop for acceptance as a candidate for diaconal ordination.[2]

Propaedeutic period

183.   Those responsible for the aspirant path in formation should be thoroughly familiar with the doctrinal understanding of the diaconate: including its ministry and life and the dimensions of formation, as described in the *Basic Norms for the Formation of Permanent Deacons* and this *Directory.* These components converge on a common goal: to enable the aspirant to demonstrate the possibility of a diaconal vocation and an appropriate level of readiness for eventual selection into candidate formation.[3]

The goal of aspirant formation

184.   To create an environment conducive to adult Christian formation, the director of formation should prepare an aspirant handbook that details the components of the program, provides a rationale and guidance for assessment, and clearly delineates the expectations and responsibilities of the aspirant, including those regarding the wife of a married aspirant. This handbook is to be approved by the bishop.[4]

Aspirant handbook

185.   Because of the aspirant's secular employment and personal and family commitments, appropriate attention is to be given to the implementation of a family life perspective in organizing the aspirant path. In this regard, the most common formation models that have emerged in the United States organize formation meetings on various evenings, weekends, holidays, or a combination of such times. Different ways of organizing the aspirant formation path are

Aspirant path: Ordinarily one year in duration

possible.[5] Since the director of formation, in collaboration with those who share in the responsibility for formation,[6] is expected to prepare a declaration of readiness for the bishop that profiles the aspirant's personality and provides a judgment of suitability for candidate formation and ultimately ordination, the aspirant path of formation must be of an appropriate length.[7] In the diocesan churches of the United States, the aspirant path of formation will ordinarily last one year.

A distinctive program

186.   Although some aspects of the aspirant path may be linked with other lay apostolate formation programs in a diocese, the aspirant path must be a distinctive program that provides for a thorough discernment of a diaconal vocation. Therefore, it must provide an appropriate initiation into diaconal spirituality; supervised pastoral experiences, especially among the poor and marginalized; and an adequate assessment of the aspirant's potential to be promoted to candidate formation, and ultimately to ordination. The aspirant path also must enable the formation personnel to create an environment in which a wife of a married aspirant can be appropriately prepared to give her consent to his continuation, and more essentially, to ascertain her compatibility with her husband's diaconal vocation and eventual ministry.[8]

The components of the aspirant path of formation

187.   During this period of discernment, the aspirant is to be introduced to the study of theology, to a deeper knowledge of the spirituality and ministry of the deacon, and to a more attentive discernment of his call. This period is also a time to form an aspirant community with its own cycle of meetings and prayer. Finally, this period is to ensure the aspirant's regular participation in spiritual direction, to introduce him to the pastoral ministries of the diocesan Church, and to assist his family in their support of his formation.[9]

II. The Dimensions of Formation in the Aspirant Path

188.   At the aspirant level in formation, the following objectives are to be highlighted. These are presented in greater detail in Chapter Three, "Dimensions in the Formation of Deacons."

Human Dimension

189.   In his post-Synodal Apostolic Exhortation *Pastores Dabo Vobis*, Pope John Paul II quoted Proposition 21 of the 1990 Extraordinary Synod of Bishops: "The whole work of priestly formation would be deprived of its necessary foundation if it lacked a suitable human formation."[10] In a similar way, the same may be said about the human dimension of diaconal formation. The goal of a "suitable human dimension" is to help the deacon develop "his human personality in such a way that it becomes a bridge and not an obstacle for others in their meeting with Jesus Christ."[11]

Goal of human dimension

190.   The aspirant path in formation is also a time for a married aspirant and his wife to assess the quality of their relationship and consider the ramifications of his possible ordination to the diaconate for their married life. For the single aspirant, it is a time to discern his capacity and receptivity for celibacy.

A family perspective

Spiritual Dimension

191.   The aspirant path of formation must create an environment in which the individual is encouraged to grow in his personal relationship with Christ and in his commitment to the Church and its mission in the world. The goal of spiritual formation is "putting on the mind of Christ," thereby establishing and nurturing attitudes, habits, and practices that provide a foundation for the development of an authentic and ongoing spiritual life.

Goal of spiritual dimension

192.   Although the fact that the wife of the married aspirant is not seeking ordination is clearly understood, nevertheless, their marriage and family are involved in the discernment of his diaconal vocation. The aspirant and his wife need to realistically assess how her own life, Church service, and family are affected and respected. The enrichment and deepening of the reciprocal and sacrificial love between husband and wife constitutes perhaps the most meaningful way the wife of the aspirant is involved in the discernment of her husband's vocation.[12]

193.   The aspirant formation community plays a significant role in spiritual formation. The aspirant path should include the following:

Content of spiritual dimension

a.   Regular celebration of the Eucharist, Liturgy of the Hours, and the Sacrament of Reconciliation
b.   Time scheduled for private prayer, meditation, and *lectio divina*
c.   Devotions to the Virgin Mary and saints
d.   Conferences and workshops on the meaning of authentic obedience, celibacy, and simplicity of life
e.   Conferences on a Christian witness in both matrimonial and celibate life to the Church and world
f.   An understanding and appreciation of the diaconal vocation, with an ability to articulate this call through the primary ministries of word, liturgy, and charity
g.   An introduction and experience of the spiritual writings of our Catholic tradition

Spiritual direction

194.   The aspirant's spiritual director is critical to the formation process. This priest, who is to be approved by the bishop, must be well trained and knowledgeable about the diaconate. The spiritual director accompanies, supports, and challenges the aspirant in his ongoing conversion. The spiritual director assists the aspirant in his relationship with God and his understanding that it is Christ who "calls," the Church that affirms his diaconal vocation, and the bishop who responds to that affirmation by the imposition of hands.

Parish and pastor

195.   As collaborators in discerning the readiness of the aspirant to move into candidate formation, the parish and its pastor also should accompany the aspirant and his family through their prayers, support, and presence. In the aspirant path in formation, the parish is the primary place to observe the aspirant's relational skills and his practice in pastoral service. The pastor, therefore, is to provide an assessment of the aspirant and his family. This assessment will further enable the formation staff to support and challenge the aspirant's discernment of his readiness to move into candidate formation.

Intellectual Dimension

Academic objectives and content

196.   The objectives and content for intellectual formation at the aspirant level should communicate a deeper knowledge of the faith and church tradition than the aspirant has already attained. It would be appropriate to promote an in-depth and systematic study of the *Catechism of the Catholic Church*, and to introduce the traditions of Catholic philosophy, spirituality, and doctrine, especially the

doctrinal understanding of the diaconate, and the threefold ministry of the deacon. The aspirant also should be taught how to participate in a theological reflection group and how to develop his ability to apply the Church's teaching on moral matters, including her social teaching, to the pressing moral questions that emerge in pastoral ministry. Such intellectual pursuits assist those responsible for formation in assessing the aspirant's readiness for the academic rigors of candidate formation. Further, he should be made aware of the needs of the people of the diocesan Church, as well as of his own parish, and be made to understand *diakonia* as a descriptive word for the mission of the Church in the world. Workshops on family issues, personal health, time management, caregiving skills, and married and celibate spirituality all contribute to an aspirant's human, spiritual, and intellectual formation.

Pastoral Dimension

197.   The focus of the pastoral dimension in the aspirant path in formation is ultimately the discernment of the aspirant's gifts for the threefold ministry of word, liturgy, and charity, and of his capacity to make a lifelong commitment to these ministries. It also enables an assessment of his wife and family in their readiness to give consent and support to his vocation and ministry. Pastoral formation should introduce the aspirant to the practical services provided by the diocesan Church. Pastoral placements, matched to the aspirant's experience and need, allow an exploration of core issues regarding charity and the social dimension of the Gospel as confronted by the diocesan Church. Exemplary deacons, approved by the bishop, should serve as mentors inviting the aspirant to accompany, observe, co-minister, and reflect upon the specific diaconal ministries experienced.[13] Appropriate ecumenical pastoral experiences should be considered and implemented as opportunities emerge. Opportunities should also be provided, when possible, for involvement with the Jewish community and with representatives of other religions.

Discernment: The ultimate focus of the pastoral dimension in formation

III. Assessment for Nomination into the Candidate Path in Formation

198.   The conclusion of the aspirant path of formation is determined through a formal assessment conducted by the committee on admission and scrutinies. This occurs when the aspirant (with the

consent of his wife, if married), with the express permission of those responsible for his formation, makes a written petition to the bishop for admission to candidacy.

Required documentation

199.   When the decision to petition for candidacy is determined, the following documents are to be prepared:

a.   A personal, handwritten, and signed letter prepared for the diocesan bishop by the aspirant requesting admission to the candidate path of formation, as well as the reception of the Rite of Admission to Candidacy[14]
b.   A personal, handwritten, and signed letter of consent prepared by the married aspirant's wife[15]

Interviews

200.   Each petitioner will be interviewed by the committee on admission and scrutinies to appraise his readiness for nomination into the candidate path of formation. The committee will also meet with the wife of a married aspirant to ascertain her level of consent and support for her husband's promotion into candidate formation. Finally, the committee will review all pertinent data on the aspirant.[16] The vote of each member and the rationale for the vote is to be recorded. The director of formation, on behalf of the committee, will prepare "a declaration which outlines the profile of the [aspirant's personality] . . . and a judgment of suitability."[17] This declaration, accompanied by the individual vote and rationale of each member of the committee, is prepared for the bishop, who selects those to be admitted to candidate formation. A copy of both the declaration and the bishop's letter to the aspirant regarding his acceptance into candidacy is placed in the petitioner's personal file.[18]

IV. The Rite of Admission to Candidacy

201.   Since entrance into the clerical state is deferred until ordination to the diaconate, the Rite of Admission to Candidacy is to be celebrated as soon as possible after the aspirant is admitted. In this rite, the one who aspires to ordination publicly manifests his will to offer himself to God and the Church to exercise a sacred order. In this way, he is admitted into the ranks of candidates for the diaconate.[19] "Enrollment among the candidates for the diaconate does not constitute any right necessarily to receive diaconal ordination.

It is a first official recognition of the positive signs of the vocation to the diaconate, which must be confirmed in the subsequent years of formation."[20]

202.   Because of its public character and its ecclesial significance, this rite should be celebrated in a proper manner, preferably on a Sunday or feast day. Special consideration should be given to the inclusion of the candidate's wife and children, as well as to the cultural traditions represented.

203.   Those accepted for candidacy—and, if married, their wives—should prepare themselves for the reception of the rite through a spiritual retreat.[21] It will usually be helpful for wives to participate in the retreat, although during portions of the retreat it will usually be helpful to provide the opportunity for separate treatment of the respective roles of each in the vocation of the husband to the diaconate. After the celebration of the Rite of Admission to Candidacy, a certificate indicating the reception, date, place, and the name of the presiding prelate must be prepared and signed by the chancellor and officially sealed. This document is to be maintained carefully in the candidate's personal file and recorded in the diocesan book on ministries and ordinations.[22]

NORMS

1.   The aspirant path is primarily a time to discern the readiness of the aspirant to be nominated to the diocesan bishop for acceptance into the candidate path in diaconal formation. (182)
2.   A handbook should be available to aspirants detailing the components of the program, rationale and guidance for assessment, and the expectations and responsibilities of the aspirants, including the wife of a married aspirant. (184)
3.   The aspirant phase, which will ordinarily last one year, involves discernment with emphasis on spiritual readiness, intellectual capacity, and pastoral abilities. (185)
4.   The aspirant path must create an environment in which the wife of a married aspirant can give her consent to her husband's continuance in formation. More essentially, it must ascertain her compatibility with her husband's diaconal vocation and eventual ministry. (186)

5. The objectives and content for intellectual formation at the aspirant level should communicate a deeper knowledge of the faith and church tradition, as well as diaconal theology and spirituality, and should include meetings for prayer, instructions, and moments of reflection that will ensure the objective nature of vocational discernment. (196)

6. The conclusion of the aspirant path in formation is determined through a formal assessment conducted by the committee on admission and scrutinies. (198)

7. After the aspirant path is completed, the aspirant is selected by the diocesan bishop. The aspirant then begins the candidate path in formation with the Rite of Admission to Candidacy, which is to be celebrated as soon as possible and in a proper manner. (201)

8. A retreat should precede the Rite of Admission to Candidacy. (203)

9. A certificate indicating the reception, date, place, and the name of the presiding prelate must be prepared and signed by the chancellor and officially sealed. This document is to be maintained carefully in the candidate's personal file and recorded in the diocesan book on ministries and ordinations. (203)

NOTES

1   BNFPD, nos. 41-44. "With admission among the aspirants to diaconate there begins a propaedeutic period . . . [in which] the aspirants will be introduced to a deeper knowledge of theology, of spirituality and of the ministry of deacon and they will be led to a more attentive discernment of their call." The propaedeutic period may be compared to the pre-seminary program in priestly formation or postulancy in religious life.

2   Ibid.

3   Cf. CL, 1-2.

4   BNFPD, no. 16.

5   BNFPD, no. 51.

6   Ibid., no. 44 (formation team, supervisors, and pastor).

7   Ibid., nos. 41, 44.

8   Ibid., no. 37.

9   Ibid., nos. 41-44.

10   PDV, no. 43.

11   Ibid.

12   ADUS.

13   Ibid., no. 22.

14   The aspirant should state his motivation and reasons for the requests; if he is married, he should indicate his awareness of the impact of diaconal ordination and ministry on his marriage and family; he also must state that he has received the consent of his wife; if he is not married, he should indicate his awareness of the meaning of diaconal ordination and ministry, as well as his understanding of and ability to live the requirement of perpetual celibacy.

15   CL, Enclosure I, 14. The wife must declare her consent for his petition to enter into candidacy formation; she also should clearly state her understanding of the meaning of diaconal ordination and ministry and its impact on their marriage and family.

16   The following assessments are to be conducted, some annually, and maintained in the aspirant's and candidate's permanent file:

    a.   Written pastoral supervisors' assessments and reports

    b.   Written parochial assessments prepared by the pastor and parish staff

    c.   If applicable, a written assessment of the rector of any previous house of formation, or a similar report from the director of diaconal formation in which the aspirant or candidate previously participated

    d.   In a case where an aspirant comes from another diocesan church, a letter of recommendation from his previous pastor is to be obtained, as well as consultation with that church's vocation and diaconate offices

    e.   An assessment of the aspirant's or candidate's aptitude for preaching, catechizing, and evangelization

f.   A personal assessment from the director of formation is to be prepared for the committee on admission and scrutinies, making use of the model prescribed by the Congregation for Divine Worship and the Discipline of the Sacraments (CL, Enclosure V).

17   BNFPD, no. 44.

18   CL, Enclosure III, especially 4, 6, and 8.

19   Pope Paul VI, Apostolic Letter, *Ministeria Quaedam* (August 15, 1972).

20   BNFPD, no. 48.

21   Ibid., no. 47.

22   CL, Enclosure I.

CHAPTER SIX

CANDIDATE PATH IN DIACONAL FORMATION

I. Introduction

204. The candidate path in diaconal formation is the occasion for continued discernment of a diaconal vocation and immediate preparation for ordination. Throughout this path in formation, the candidate himself assumes the primary responsibility for his discernment and development.[1]

> Self-formation does not imply isolation . . . or independence from formators, but responsibility and dynamism in responding with generosity to God's call, valuing to the highest the people and tools which Providence puts at one's disposition. Self-formation has its roots in a firm determination to grow in life according to the Spirit and in conformity with the vocation received. . . .[2]

II. The Length of the Candidate Path in Formation

205. In accord with the Code of Canon Law, the *Basic Norms for the Formation of Permanent Deacons* by the Congregation for Catholic Education specifies that the candidate path in diaconal formation "must last at least three years, in addition to the *propaedeutic period*, for all candidates."[3] Readiness for ordination is assessed annually by both the candidate and formation personnel to ascertain what level of achievement the candidate has reached in his understanding of the diaconal vocation, its responsibilities, and its obligations; his growth in the spiritual life; his competency in required diaconal knowledge and skills; his practical experience in pastoral ministry; and his witness of human and affective maturity. If he is married, an appraisal of his wife's readiness and consent is also to be made. In a Circular Letter directed to diocesan ordinaries on assessing the readiness of candidates for ordination, the Congregation for Divine Worship and the Discipline of the Sacraments recalls that "St. Paul's

"Do not be hasty in the laying-on of hands."

admonition remains true for the Church today, as it did in his own time: '*Do not be hasty in the laying-on of hands.*'"[4]

Candidate path in formation: An integral and substantive program

206.   Regarding the precise number of hours for lectures, seminars, and related educational activities specified in the *Basic Norms for the Formation of Permanent Deacons*,[5] the objective is to guarantee the planning and implementation of an integral and substantive program of formation that adequately prepares a candidate to represent the Church as a deacon. A substantive program includes not only class preparation, participation, and attendance, but also seminars, workshops, field education projects, theological reflection, shared opportunities for spiritual growth (e.g., liturgical celebrations and prayer, spiritual conferences, retreats), individual spiritual direction, and other formation experiences. Diocesan compliance with this requirement and others as specified in the *Basic Norms for the Formation of Permanent Deacons* and in this *Directory* may be verified by the review of its formation program by the Bishops' Committee on the Diaconate (see Appendix I).

III. Formation Environments

207.   The communities in which the candidate participates influence the formation process.[6] Those entrusted with formation must take care to assess these environments as resources for discerning, supporting, and nurturing a diaconal vocation.

Candidate Formation Community

Adult experience

208.   The candidate community should become primarily an integrating experience where dialogue and collaborative activity provide a unique opportunity for adults to discern the activity of the Holy Spirit in their lives and experiences.

Candidate handbook

209.   To create an environment conducive to adult Christian formation, the director of formation should prepare a candidate handbook that details the components of the program; provides the rationale, criteria, and guidance for assessments, especially regarding readiness for institution into the ministries of lector and acolyte, and ultimately, for ordination to the diaconate; and clearly delineates the expectations and responsibilities of the candidate, including the wife of a married candidate. This handbook is to be approved by the bishop.[7]

The Community of Deacons

210.   The community of deacons can be a "precious support in the discernment of vocation, in human growth, in the initiation to the spiritual life, in theological study and pastoral experience."[8] Scheduled opportunities for conversation and shared pastoral experiences between a candidate and deacon, as well as meetings between the wife of a candidate and the wife of a deacon can mutually sustain their enthusiasm and realism about the diaconate. Some deacons should be appointed by the bishop to serve as mentors to individual candidates or a small group of candidates.[9]

The role of the ordained community

The Parish Community

211.   The parish community is an essential extension of the formation community. Through its prayer and support, the parish "makes the faithful aware of this ministry, [and] gives to the candidate a strong aid to his vocational discernment."[10]

The parish community

The Family Community

212.   The family is the primary community accompanying the candidate on the formative journey. For married candidates, the communion of life and love, established by the marriage covenant and consecrated by the Sacrament of Matrimony, offers a singular contribution to the formation process.[11] The single candidate's family also contributes to his formation; those responsible for implementing the formation process should consult with the single candidate to ascertain the strength of his support from his family and friends to ensure that his vocation is also encouraged and fostered.

The family formation community

The Marketplace Community

213.   Those responsible for implementing the formation process are to thoroughly determine the impact of the candidate's employment situation—his *marketplace* formation community—on his preparation, discernment, and readiness for ordination to the diaconate. Pope John Paul II stressed the importance of this particular formation environment at the plenary assembly of the Congregation for the Clergy: "It is the circumstances of his life—prudently evaluated by the candidate himself and by the bishop, before ordination—which should, if necessary, be adapted to the exercise of his ministry by facilitating it in every way."[12]

Circumstances of life prudently evaluated

IV. The Dimensions of Formation in the Candidate Path

214.   Those responsible for the candidate path in formation should be thoroughly familiar with the doctrinal understanding of the diaconate, the ministry and life of deacons, the dimensions of formation, and the discernment of a diaconal vocation described earlier in this *Directory*. These components have a common goal: to enable the candidate to demonstrate an appropriate level of preparedness for nomination to the diocesan bishop for ordination to the diaconate. The following descriptions highlight specific components to be emphasized.

Human Dimension

Development of human qualities | 215.   The aim of the human dimension of the candidate path in formation is to continue to build on the human qualities already discerned during the aspirancy period (see paragraphs 189 and 190 above), developing them and adding necessary skills for an effective and responsible diaconal ministry. Emphasis needs to be placed upon his relational and collaborative qualities and skills, especially his strengths and limitations in this regard. During the candidate path, the candidate also needs to acknowledge his giftedness and to develop the habit of authentic self-criticism in light of the Gospel. He must learn how to balance his personal, familial, work, and ministerial responsibilities.

Spiritual Dimension

216.   One of the primary objectives of the spiritual dimension of the candidate path in formation is "to assist the candidate in achieving a spiritual integration" of his life, family, work, and apostolic service.[13] The candidate, therefore, should be thoroughly introduced to the theology and spirituality of work as both a vocation and an apostolate, as well as a profession. The spiritual goal is for the candidate to increase in holiness by "equipping and motivating" him to lay a foundation upon which he may "continue [his] spiritual growth after ordination." Throughout his formation, the candidate is "to secure the assistance of a . . . [priest spiritual director], to cultivate regular patterns of prayer and sacramental participation, and . . . to reflect spiritually on [his] ministry."[14] It would also be useful for small groups of candidates to engage together in theological reflection "on the challenges and opportunities of their ministries"

in relationship to the Gospel and magisterial teaching.[15] Further, throughout the formation process, it is expedient that the candidate's spiritual director and those responsible for his formation ascertain the candidate's understanding, willingness, and capacity to accept the Church's discipline regarding perpetual celibacy not merely among those who are not married but, also, among married men who will be required to embrace this ecclesiastical discipline in widowhood or divorce (even with a subsequent annulment). Dispensations from the requirement of celibacy cannot be presumed. Continuation in ministry cannot be presumed even with the reception of the requested dispensation.

217.   The goals of the spiritual dimension during the candidate path in formation include the following:

Spiritual goals

a.   To help each candidate to increase in holiness by deepening and cultivating his commitment to Christ and the Church
b.   To assist the candidate in discerning whether he has a vocation to the diaconate
c.   To help him deepen his prayer life, personal, familial, communal, and liturgical; and to instill in the candidate a commitment to pray daily for the Church, especially through the Liturgy of the Hours
d.   To strengthen the personal charisms he has already demonstrated in his life
e.   To help him integrate his new commitment to prepare for the diaconate with his previous commitments to his family and professional employment
f.   To acquaint him with the relationship between spirituality and his commitment to the Church's ministry of charity and justice
g.   To acquaint him with Catholic classical and contemporary spiritual writings and the witness of the saints
h.   To prepare him for the challenges of spiritual leadership that his ministry will entail

Intellectual Dimension

218.   The intellectual dimension of the candidate path in formation should be carefully designed. A description of the core content for the candidate can be found in Norms 5-12 at the end of this chapter. The intellectual dimension is "oriented toward ministry,

Intellectual goals

providing the candidate with the knowledge and appreciation of the faith that he needs in order to carry out his ministry"[16] of word, liturgy, and charity. The course of study should be complete and must be in harmony with the magisterial teaching of the Church so that the future deacon is a "reliable witn[ess] of the faith and spokes[man] for the Church's teaching."[17] It should also take into account the specific diaconal services the candidate will provide in the communities that he will be appointed to serve, as well as topics that reflect the specific concerns of the Church in the United States. The intellectual dimension must equip the candidate for his leadership and participation in the new evangelization and for his effective heralding of the Gospel in today's society. The study of sacred Scripture, liturgy, evangelization, and missiology are to be given prominence.

Pastoral Dimension

Pastoral placement and supervision

219.   "During formation, engagement in a wide diversity of" pastoral field education placements, "at least on a limited basis, will not only give the candidate a greater awareness of the needs and mission of the [diocesan] Church, but will assist in the discernment and development of his own . . . talents and gifts."[18] These pastoral field education experiences "should provide an opportunity for theological reflection, as well as occasions to translate" intellectual knowledge into pastoral service.[19] A description of the core content for the formation of candidates can be found in Norms 13-15 at the end of this chapter. "Competent, objective, and" supportive supervisors will be required in order to achieve these goals.[20] The diocesan Church "must be committed to the [selection and] preparation of skillful . . . supervisors who possess pastoral experience, [training] . . . in the art of supervision, and . . . [the ability to assist] mature men with [diverse] life experiences. . . ."[21] During candidacy, emphasis also should be given to the study of the role of culture in human, spiritual, and pastoral formation. Further, the pastoral dimension should provide a significant grounding in the social justice teaching of the Church.

V. The Assessment of Candidates

Academic Assessment

Measurement of achievement in a pastoral setting

220.   A primary opportunity for assessment of the candidate would be within an actual pastoral setting. Can the candidate do that which his training is preparing him to do? Does the way in which he

presents himself in pastoral ministry show, for example, an integrated and balanced sense of the ecclesiology of the Second Vatican Council and an understanding of his role within the Church and in its mission of service? Does the way he participates in and leads prayerful gatherings of his community give evidence of liturgical knowledge and cultural sensitivity? Can he demonstrate a properly formed conscience and moral sensitivity? Can he form others in a convincing, sound manner?

221.   Another assessment option is theological reflection on his pastoral practice. Here the role of the peer community is of utmost importance. The candidate reports on his field education experience and the community enables him to reflect upon the human, spiritual, intellectual, and pastoral dimensions of his actions. This format greatly fosters the sense of partnership in assessment.

Theological reflection

222.   Another opportunity for assessment lies in the classroom imitation of pastoral practice, whether through case study, role playing, or some form of pastoral problem solving. Although not empowered by the sense of immediacy or by connection to a real incident, such simulations can be designed to explore any number of competencies in a structured and progressive program.

Pastoral simulation

223.   For the assessment of the candidate's intellectual formation, traditional examinations or academic papers are necessary, as prescribed by the *Basic Norms for the Formation of Permanent Deacons* of the Congregation for Catholic Education.

Traditional examinations

224.   A sense of partnership can be fostered by allowing the candidate to present a portfolio of his accomplishments, to design a variety of ways in which he may demonstrate his readiness, or to engage in a collaborative study venture with those charged with his formation.

Independent study

225.   A comprehensive and integrative seminar, such as those used in professional education, is recommended as a model to determine the level of assimilation and achievement of the candidate at the completion of his theological course of study. This model fulfills the requirement of a comprehensive review as required by the *Basic Norms for the Formation of Permanent Deacons*.[22] The faculty facilitators of the seminar evaluate how effectively the individual candidate

Comprehensive and integrative seminar at the conclusion of the course of study

is "able to explain his faith and bring to maturity a lively ecclesial conscience,"[23] how he has acquired "the capacity to read a situation and an adequate inculturation of the Gospel,"[24] and how successfully he has used "communication techniques and group dynamics, the ability to speak in public, and [the ability] to give guidance and counsel."[25] In such seminars, typically formatted around case studies of a pastoral nature, the candidate has an opportunity to explore pastoral solutions in the presence of his peers, formation faculty, and pastoral supervisors. In the seminar, he is called upon not only to demonstrate an intellectual understanding of theology, but also its application in pastoral practice. He gives and receives feedback, thus demonstrating his competency in such areas as communication and his ability to work constructively within a group. In addition, his pastoral world view is exposed and assessed and his "pastoral intuition" is honored and challenged. The goal of this comprehensive and integrative seminar is always to project how the candidate will live a diaconal lifestyle and ministry.

Vocational Assessment

Regular evaluation meetings

226.   Interviews should be scheduled regularly with the candidates and their families, their pastors and pastoral supervisors, members of the faculty, and mentors. The director of formation and those who collaborate with him should gather at regularly scheduled times to stay informed about a candidate's progress. They should address concerns and become collectively aware of their common collaborative role in assisting, counseling, and assessing the candidate. This responsibility should be regarded as their most important task. Due care must be taken, however, to preserve the confidentiality of spiritual direction in these proceedings.

Annual written report for the bishop

227.   The responsibility of formation personnel culminates in the preparation of a yearly written report on each candidate. This report, which is to be presented to the diocesan bishop, provides a synthesis of the candidate's achievements and limitations, particularly in reference to his human, spiritual, intellectual, and pastoral readiness for continuation in the formation process and, ultimately, for nomination to ordination.[26] The written report is to be maintained in the candidate's personal file, where accumulated reports can be compared to ascertain patterns of growth or regression, as well as new areas for affirmation or concern.

228.   The director of formation must transmit this report verbally to the candidate. It should be made available to the candidate's spiritual director, whose "task is that of discerning the workings of the Spirit in the soul of those called and, at that same time, of accompanying and supporting their ongoing conversion."[27] It may be helpful to share the report with the candidate's pastor, if he did not participate in the formal review. Finally, the director of formation also will share this report with the committee on admission and scrutinies, especially in its deliberations regarding admittance to the ministries of lector and acolyte, and ordination to the diaconate.

Other recipients of the report

229.   If a candidate does not possess the necessary human, spiritual, intellectual, or pastoral qualities that will allow him to minister as a deacon in a collaborative and effective way, it is only just to the individual and to the Church to communicate this to him as early as possible and in a constructive manner. Sometimes the evaluation consensus clearly indicates termination of formation or a refusal of recommendation for ordination. Candidates who lack positive qualities for continuing in the formation process should not nourish false hopes and illusions that could damage themselves and their families, their peers, or the Church. Therefore, with the approval of the diocesan bishop, the candidate should be advised to leave formation. Although no one has a right to continue in formation or a right to be ordained, in justice and with pastoral sensitivity the reasons for this decision should be shared with the candidate, and a fair hearing should be given to his own assessment of the situation, as well as to that of others who may wish to speak on his behalf.

Dismissal from formation

230.   In situations of doubt about the readiness of a candidate to be called to ordination or about his progress in achieving appropriate levels of adult formation, the diocesan bishop may consider a period of probation. This time, however, should be specifically limited, not left open-ended. Likewise, appropriate supervision is absolutely necessary during this period to bring about needed growth and provide suitable information on which to base a judgment. It will be helpful, therefore, to prepare a written plan of action indicating the goals to be achieved, the actions that will be followed to meet the goals, and the means of evaluating and verifying the achievement of the goals. This written plan should further specify the supervisor who will accompany the candidate through the process. It must be understood

Leave of absence

that in such situations, the burden of proof of readiness for ordination rests with the candidate, and doubt is resolved in favor of the Church.

231.   Paralleling the process indicated for the external forum, spiritual direction is similarly crucial to the candidate's discernment. The individual's spiritual director should receive the information regarding this period of probation, and through internal forum, he should assist the individual through regularly scheduled meetings.

VI. Scrutinies for Installation into the Ministries of Lector and Acolyte and Ordination to the Diaconate

Canonical requirements prior to ordination

232.   In accord with the Circular Letter from the Congregation for Divine Worship and the Discipline of the Sacraments, scrutinies are to take place prior to installation into the ministries of lector and acolyte[28] and prior to ordination to the diaconate.[29]

233.   A collegial session of the committee on admission and scrutinies is to be scheduled for these assessments.[30] Having consulted the committee, the bishop will select those to be admitted to the specific ministry and those to be called to ordination.

Rite of Installation into the Ministry of Lector and Ministry of Acolyte

Retreat and celebration of the liturgical rite

234.   It is appropriate for a retreat or a day for reflection to precede the reception of the specific ministry. It will usually be helpful to wives to participate in the retreat, although during portions of the retreat it will usually be helpful to provide the opportunity for separate treatment of the respective roles of each in the vocation of the husband to the diaconate. The conferral of the ministry should be celebrated on a Sunday or feast day, according to the rite of *The Roman Pontifical*. These rites are public celebrations with ecclesial significance.[31] Special attention should be given to the participation of the wives and children of married candidates. The ministry of lector is to be conferred first. "It is appropriate that a certain period of time elapse between the conferring of the lectorate [rite of lector[and acolytate [rite of acolyte] in such a way that the candidate may exercise the ministry he has received."[32]

Documentation of the installation

235.   After the reception of the ministry, a certificate indicating the ministry received, date, place, and conferring prelate should be

prepared and signed by the chancellor of the diocese and officially sealed. This document is to be kept in the candidate's personal file and noted in the diocesan book of ministries and ordinations.

The Rite of Ordination to the Diaconate

236.   An interval of at least six months must elapse between the conferring of the ministry of acolyte and ordination to the dia-conate.[33] Further, a canonical retreat must precede the ordination.[34] It will usually be helpful to wives to participate in the retreat, although during portions of the retreat it will usually be helpful to provide the opportunity for separate treatment of the respective roles of each in the vocation of the husband to the diaconate. Prior to ordination to the diaconate, the ordinand must make the Profession of the Faith in the presence of the bishop or his delegate and must sign it by his own hand. He must take the Oath of Fidelity and make a personal declaration concerning his freedom to receive sacred ordination, as well as his own clear awareness of the obligations and commitments implied by that ordination. An unmarried candi-date must make a declaration regarding the obligation of sacred celibacy; this declaration must be written in the candidate's own handwriting and expressed in his own words. All of these documents are to be carefully preserved in the candidate's personal file.[35]

Six-month interval between installation and ordination

237.   It is preferable to celebrate the ordination in the cathedral church on a Sunday or feast day, according to the rite of *The Roman Pontifical*, inviting the diocesan Church's full participation. "During the rite special attention should be given to the participation of the wives and children of the married ordinands."[36]

238.   After the ordination, a certificate should be prepared con-taining the date, place, and name of the ordaining prelate. It should be signed and sealed by the chancellor. This information also should be recorded in the diocesan book of ministries and ordinations. The certificate, together with the letter of petition and the bishop's letter of call to ordination, should be enclosed in the newly ordained's per-sonal and permanent file. This file should be transferred as soon after the ordination as is convenient from the formation office to a permanent location among the curia records in the diocesan chancery. The director of formation or someone designated by the bishop should also notify the church in which the newly ordained

Curia and parish records

was baptized so that the information regarding the ordination may be included in that church's baptismal-sacramental records. The parish of Baptism should notify the director of formation when the information has been recorded.[37]

NORMS

1. The candidate path in formation must last at least three years in addition to the aspirant path. (205)

2. Regarding the number of hours of lectures, seminars, and related educational activities specified in the *Basic Norms for the Formation of Permanent Deacons*, the objective of this requirement is to guarantee the planning and implementation of an integral and substantive program of formation that adequately prepares a candidate to represent the Church as an ordained minister. (206)

3. The human dimension of this path in formation continues to develop the human qualities already discerned during the aspirant path, adding necessary skills for an effective and responsible diaconal ministry. (215)

4. The spiritual dimension of this path happens through the candidate's meeting regularly with his spiritual director and those responsible for formation. The goals are for the candidate to increase in holiness; to deepen his prayer life through the Eucharist, the Sacrament of Reconciliation, the Liturgy of the Hours, and devotions; and to acquaint himself with the Catholic spiritual tradition reflected in classic and modern spiritual writings. (216, 217)

5. The intellectual dimension of this path in formation introduces the candidate to the essentials of Christian doctrine and practice, including the core areas of theology faithful to the Magisterium of the Church and based on Scripture and Tradition, the documents of the Second Vatican Council, the *Catechism of the Catholic Church*, and the *General Directory for Catechesis*. (218, 124)

6. From Scripture, the core studies should include the major themes and content of the Old and New Testaments: Christian Scriptures, their stages of formation, and their place at the heart of Scripture. Attention should be given to the biblical

themes of justice and peace that root and foster Catholic social teaching. (124)

7. From dogmatic theology, the core studies should include fundamental theology, God as trinity, christology, creation and the nature of sin, redemption, grace and the human person, ecclesiology (both the Latin and Eastern Catholic Churches), ecumenism and interreligious dialogue, sacraments (especially the Sacrament of Holy Orders and the theology and the relationship of the diaconate to the episcopate, the presbyterate, and the laity), eschatology, Mariology, missiology, and Catholic evangelization. (124)

8. From moral theology, the core studies should include fundamental moral theology, medical-moral ethics, sexuality, and social-ministerial ethics. The social teaching of the Church should be presented substantially. (124)

9. From historical studies, the candidate should be introduced to the history of the Church through the ages with an emphasis on patristics. The candidates should be familiar with the multicultural origins of the Church in the United States. (124)

10. From Canon Law, the core studies should include a general introduction and those canons specific to the exercise of the diaconate, in particular, marriage legislation, as well as the obligations and rights of clerics. (124)

11. From spirituality, the core studies should include an introduction to spirituality, to spiritual direction, and to a selection of classic spiritual writers. (124)

12. From liturgy, the core studies should include an introduction to liturgy and to the historical, spiritual, and juridical aspects of liturgy. (124)

13. Practica for the ministry of liturgy should include specific training in the functions of the deacon during the Eucharist, Baptism, RCIA, marriage, the rites of Christian burial, and other liturgical ministries of the diaconate. (130)

14. From homiletics, deacons should have courses specifically aimed at preparing and delivering homilies. (130)

15. Pastoral formation must include a wide diversity of pastoral services, including opportunities for theological reflection. Attention should be given to the study of the role of culture in human and spiritual formation. (219)

16. A comprehensive seminar should be conducted at the end of the candidate path of formation to enhance the candidates' integration of learning and to assess their readiness for ordination. (225)

17. The responsibility of formation personnel culminates in the preparation of a yearly written report on each aspirant and candidate that will be presented to the diocesan bishop through the director of formation. (227)

18. The director of formation must verbally transmit a yearly report to each candidate. (228)

19. Scrutinies are to take place prior to installation into the ministries of lector and acolyte and prior to ordination to the diaconate. (232)

20. A retreat or day of reflection should precede the reception of the ministries of lector and acolyte. (234)

21. An interval of at least six months must elapse between the conferring of the ministry of acolyte and ordination to the diaconate. (236)

22. A canonical retreat must precede ordination. (236)

23. After the installation into each ministry and after ordination, a certificate should be prepared containing the date, place, and name of the installing/ordaining prelate. It should be signed and sealed by the chancellor. This information also should be recorded in the diocesan book of ministries and ordinations. The director of formation should also notify the church in which the newly ordained was baptized so that the information regarding the ordination may be included in that church's baptismal-sacramental records. The parish of Baptism should notify the director of formation when the information has been recorded. All of these canonical documents should be transferred as soon after the ordination as is convenient from the formation office to a permanent location among the curia records in the diocesan chancery.

NOTES

1   BNFPD, no. 28.

2   Ibid.

3   Ibid., nos. 49-50, italics added; cf. CIC, c. 236.

4   CL, 9, citing 1 Tm 5:22.

5   BNFPD, no. 82.

6   Ibid., no. 26.

7   Ibid., no. 16.

8   Ibid., no. 26.

9   Ibid., no. 22.

10   BNFPD, no. 27.

11   Ibid.

12   PDO, no. 4.

13   PDG (1984), no. 94.

14   Ibid., no. 99.

15   Ibid., no. 99.

16   Ibid., no. 75.

17   Ibid., no. 78.

18   Ibid., no. 84.

19   Ibid.

20   Ibid.

21   Ibid., no. 85.

22   BNFPD, no. 82.

23   Ibid., no. 80.

24   Ibid.

25   Ibid.

26   This written assessment should include an estimation of an unmarried candidate's capacity to lead a perpetual chaste and celibate life. For a married candidate, it should present an appraisal of his family's stability and capacity to support his vocation, especially addressing the status of his wife's consent and her own integrity. Each year, the number of affirmative and negative votes of the formation team and faculty regarding the continuance or separation of the candidate from formation is to be recorded. If there are abstentions, they are to be explained (CL, Enclosure III, 7, 8). The diocesan bishop expects the objective and critical judgment of those who collaborate with him in formation. This report should reflect a clear consensus among those who have been involved with the candidate's training and formation.

27   BNFPD, no. 23.

28   CL, Enclosures II, III. Required documentation and procedures for institution into the ministries of lector and acolyte include the following (these are to be followed when

petitioning for institution into the ministry of lector and repeated when petitioning for the ministry of acolyte):

a.   The candidate handwrites his request to be admitted to the specific ministry. This request must be composed by the candidate personally, written out in his own hand; it "may not be copied formulary, or worse, a photocopied text" (CL, Enclosure II, 1)

b.   The director of formation prepares a personal report, which should be detailed, making use of the model found in CL, Enclosure V, and which should include the candidate's annual self and peer assessments

c.   The candidate's pastor is consulted, and he writes a letter of recommendation

d.   The committee on admission and scrutinies interviews the candidate's wife, if he is married, to ascertain her understanding of her husband's institution into these ministries as part of the formation discernment process

e.   Faculty and pastoral field supervisors provide assessments of the candidate

f.   A smaller team from the committee on admission and scrutinies interviews the candidate to ascertain his knowledge of the ministry to be received and his capacity to fulfill its responsibilities

g.   Other documentation is provided, as requested by the committee (CL, Enclosure II)

29   Required documentation and procedures for ordination to the diaconate include the following (these are to be followed when petitioning for ordination to the diaconate):

a.   Before petitioning for ordination, the candidate keeps in mind that there must be an interval of at least six months between the conferring of the ministry of acolyte and ordination to the diaconate (CIC, c. 1035:2)

b.   The candidate submits a written request to be admitted to the Order of Deacons. This request must be composed by the candidate personally, written out in his own hand; it "may not be copied formulary, or worse, a photocopied text" (CL, Enclosure II, 1)

c.   The candidate's wife writes and signs a statement in which she declares her consent to the ordination petition of her husband and makes clear her own understanding of the meaning of diaconal ministry (CL, Enclosure II, 8)

d.   The director of formation prepares a personal report, which should be detailed, making use of the model proposed in CL, Enclosure V, and which should include the annual Vocational Assessment Report

e.   The director, in compliance with CIC c. 1032, must present a certificate verifying the candidate's completion of all required studies

f.   The candidate's pastor is consulted, and he writes a letter of recommendation

g.   The committee on admission and scrutinies interviews the candidate to ascertain his knowledge of the Order of Deacons to be received and its obligations and rights; his understanding and willingness, if single or widowed, to accept the Church's discipline regarding perpetual celibate chastity; his understanding and willingness, if married, to embrace the magisterial teaching on marriage and sexuality, as well as its ecclesiastical discipline in widowhood; and his understanding of the rights and obligations of a cleric and his capacity to fulfill these responsibilities

h.   The committee interviews the wife of a married candidate to ascertain her willingness to support his petition and to live as a wife of a deacon

i.   The canonical banns are published within a sufficiently extended period of time in advance of ordination in the parishes where the candidate has had an extended residence or presence in his formation ministries (CL, Enclosure II, 8; CIC, c. 1051:2)

j.   The candidate provides a recent photograph and biographical information for use in the publicizing of his ordination

k.   Other documentation is provided, as requested by the committee (CL, Enclosure IV)

"It should not be permitted that the candidate's family or the parish community presume his future Ordination" before the call of the competent authority, especially by mailing invitations or making other preparations for the ordination celebration. "Behavior of this kind can constitute a form of psychological pressure that must be avoided in every way possible (CL, Enclosure IV:3)." The bishop will select those to be ordained to the diaconate and will set the date and other specifications for the ordination. It is assumed that this will be done in consultation with the ordinand and his family.

30   The recommendation and vote on each request is to be recorded and attached to the written report submitted to the diocesan bishop. All documentation generated by the committee should be maintained. (CL)

31   BNFPD, nos. 57-59.

32   Ibid., no. 59.

33   Ibid., quoting CIC, c. 1035:2.

34   Ibid., no. 65; cf. CIC, c. 1039.

35   CL, Enclosure IV.

36   BNFPD, no. 65.

37   Cf. CIC, c. 1054.

CHAPTER SEVEN

POST-ORDINATION PATH IN DIACONAL FORMATION

I. Introduction

239.   The post-ordination path in diaconal formation "is first and foremost a process of continual conversion."[1]

Goals for post-ordination formation

[It] requires that ongoing formation strengthen in [each deacon] the consciousness and willingness to live in intelligent, active and mature communion with their bishops and priests of their diocese, and with the Supreme Pontiff who is the visible foundation of the entire Church's unity. When formed in this way, they can become in their ministry effective promoters of communion. . . . The continuing formation of deacons is a human necessity which must be seen in continuity with the divine call to serve the Church in the ministry and with the initial formation given to deacons, to the extent that these are considered two initial moments in a single, living, process of Christian and diaconal life.[2]

The goal for this path in formation is to responsibly address the various aspects of a deacon's ministry, the development of his personality and, above all, his commitment to spiritual growth. "Ongoing formation must include and harmonize all dimensions of the life and ministry of the deacon. Thus . . . it should be complete, systematic and personalized in its diverse aspects whether human, spiritual, intellectual or pastoral."[3] The primary source for post-ordination formation is the ministry itself.

The deacon matures in its exercise and by focusing his own call to holiness on the fulfillment of his social and ecclesial duties, in particular, of his ministerial functions and responsibilities. The formation of deacons should, therefore, concentrate in a special way on awareness of their ministerial character.[4]

"Do not neglect
the gift you
have [received]."

240.   The post-ordination path in formation is motivated by the same dynamism as the holy order received:

> Do not neglect the gift you have, which was conferred on you through the prophetic word with the imposition of hands. . . . Be diligent in these matters, be absorbed in them, so that your progress may be evident to everyone. Attend to yourself and to your teaching; persevere in both tasks, for by doing so you will save both yourself and those who listen to you.[5]

II. The Dimensions of Formation in the Post-Ordination Path

241.   The post-ordination path should provide the deacon with ample opportunities to continue to develop and integrate the dimensions of formation into his life and ministry.[6] In this way, the quality of his life and ministry will be ensured, avoiding the risk of ministerial burnout. In certain cases of difficulty, such as discouragement or a change in ministry, post-ordination formation can entail a process of renewal and revitalization.

Two distinct levels
of formation

242.   In designing the content for an ongoing formation program, those responsible "should take into consideration two distinct but closely related levels of formation: the diocesan level, in reference to the bishop. . . . and the community level in which the deacon exercises his own ministry, in reference to the parish priest."[7] The deacon is ordained for service to the diocesan Church, even though the focus of that service will usually be within a particular parochial community. Keeping a balance in this dual relationship is essential to his effectiveness as a deacon.

Wife and family
ongoing formation

243.   Just as the role of the wife and children needed to be carefully discerned throughout the aspirant and candidate paths in formation, this discernment is equally important in the post-ordination path. It is appropriate to recognize the importance of the ongoing formation of the wives and families of deacons and to provide formation resources and opportunities for them. A family life perspective remains an essential point of reference. Care must, however, be exercised so that "the essential distinction of roles and the clear independence of the ministry" are maintained.[8]

244.   Some deacons, because of a strong desire to function in their diaconal ministries, may dismiss valid areas of concern and conflict with their spouse and family. This dismissal is to be avoided. A married deacon and his family must be instructed on how to request help early when they experience a need. "Unfortunately, our society still focuses almost exclusively on a remedial approach; families [usually] seek help [only] after a crisis has occurred and other problems develop. An alternative is a preventive strategy."[9]

Preventive strategy

Human Dimension:
Developing "Human Qualities as Valuable Instruments for Ministry"[10]
245.   To effectively carry out his diaconal ministry, the deacon must extend himself generously in various forms of human relations without discrimination so that he is perceived by others as a credible witness to the sanctity and preciousness of human life. Post-ordination formation should enable the deacon to pursue this witness to the faith with greater effectiveness.

Spiritual Dimension: "Diaconal Spirituality"[11]
246.   In Baptism, each disciple receives the universal call to holiness. In the reception of the Sacrament of Holy Orders, the deacon receives a "new consecration to God" through which he is configured to Christ the Servant and sent to serve God's people.[12] Growth into holiness, therefore, is "a duty binding all the faithful." But "for the deacon it is has a further basis in the special consecration received. It includes the practice of the Christian virtues and the various evangelical precepts and counsels according to [his] own state of life."[13] The celibate deacon should, therefore, "be especially careful to give witness to [his] brothers and sisters by [his] fidelity to the celibate life the better to move them to seek those values consonant with man's transcendent vocation."[14] He also must be "faithful to the spiritual life and duties of [his] ministry in a spirit of prudence and vigilance, remembering that 'the spirit is willing but the flesh is weak.'"[15] For the married deacon, the Sacrament of Matrimony

is a gift from God and should be a source of nourishment for [his] spiritual life. . . . it will be necessary to integrate these various elements [i.e., family life and professional responsibilities] in a unitary fashion, especially by means of shared prayer.

In marriage, love becomes an interpersonal giving of self, a mutual fidelity, a source of new life, a support in times of joy and sorrow: in short, love becomes service. When lived in faith, this family service is for the rest of the faithful an example of the love of Christ. The married deacon must use it as a stimulus of his diakonia in the Church.[16]

To foster and nurture his diaconal ministry and lifestyle according to his state in life, each deacon must be rooted in a spirit of service that verifies "a genuine personal encounter with Jesus, a trusting dialogue with the Father, and a deep experience of the Spirit."[17]

247.   Some recommended spiritual exercises to assist the deacon in developing and promoting his spiritual life include the following:

a.   Daily or frequent participation in the Eucharist, the source and summit of the Christian life, as well as daily or frequent eucharistic adoration, as often as his secular employment and family requirements permit
b.   Regular reception of the Sacrament of Reconciliation
c.   Daily celebration of the Liturgy of the Hours, especially morning and evening prayer
d.   Shared prayer with his family
e.   Meditative prayer on the holy Scriptures—*lectio divina*
f.   Devotion to Mary, the Mother God
g.   Prayerful preparation of oneself prior to the celebration of the sacraments, preaching, or beginning one's ministry of charity
h.   Theological reflection
i.   Regular spiritual direction
j.   Participation in an annual retreat
k.   Authentic living of one's state of life
l.   Time for personal and familial growth

Intellectual Dimension: Theological Renewal[18]

248.   The intellectual dimension of diaconate formation does not end with ordination but is an ongoing requirement of the vocation. The theological demands of their call to a singular ministry of ecclesial service and pastoral servant-leadership require of deacons a growing love for the Church—for God's Holy People—shown by their faithful and competent carrying out of their proper functions

and responsibilities. The intellectual dimension of post-ordination formation must be systematic and substantive, deepening the intellectual content initially studied during the candidate path of formation. Study days, renewal courses and participation in academic institutes are appropriate formats to achieve this goal. In particular,

> it is of the greatest use and relevance to study, appropriate and diffuse the social doctrine of the Church. A good knowledge of that teaching will permit many deacons to mediate it in their different professions, at work and in their families. [It may also be useful to] the diocesan bishop [to] invite those who are capable to specialize in a theological discipline and obtain the necessary academic qualifications at those pontifical academies or institutes recognized by the Apostolic See which guarantee doctrinally correct information. . . . Ongoing formation cannot be confined simply to updating, but should seek to facilitate a practical configuration of the deacon's entire life to Christ who loves all and serves all.[19]

Pastoral Dimension:
"Pastoral Methodology for an Effective Ministry"[20]

249.   Pastoral formation constantly encourages the deacon "to perfect the effectiveness of his ministry of making the love and service of Christ present in the Church and in society without distinction, especially to the poor and to those most in need. Indeed, it is from the pastoral love of Christ that the ministry of deacons draws its model and inspiration."[21]

"For an adequate pastoral formation, it is necessary to organize encounters in which the principal objective is the reflection upon the pastoral plan of the Diocese."[22] When the diaconate is conceived from the start as an integral part of an overall pastoral plan, deacons will have a richer and firmer sense of their own identity and purpose. Thus, an ongoing pastoral formation program responds to the concerns and issues pertinent to the deacon's life and ministry, in keeping with the pastoral plan of the diocesan Church and in loyal and firm communion with the Supreme Pontiff and with his own bishop.

III. Additional Considerations

Specialization Programming

250.   "The ministry of the word leads to ministry at the altar, which in turn prompts the transformation of life by the liturgy, resulting in charity."[23] As a deacon eventually focuses on more specific ministries through his responsiveness to the growing needs of the people he serves, it will be necessary to provide more specific programming designed to address his personal needs, talents, and ministry.[24] Initially, however, consideration should be given to deepening his understanding and skills in the ministries of the word, liturgy, and charity.

Program for the Newly Ordained

First three years of diaconate ministry

251.   There are particular matters relevant to the newly ordained. It is important, therefore, that the newly ordained begin their diaconate ministry in a positive and supportive manner. A program should be planned for the first three years of their diaconate ministry[25] and coordinated by the director of deacon personnel. In the early phase of their ministry, ongoing formation will largely reinforce the basic training and its application in ministerial practice. Later formation will entail a more in-depth study of the various components proposed in the dimensions in diaconal formation. Consideration also should be given to introducing the newly ordained to a conversational study of a second language used within the diocese and the study of its cultural environment. Deacons, as ministers of Christ the Servant, should be prepared to link people of diverse languages and cultures into the local faith community of the diocese and parish. Deacons in their initial pastoral assignments should be carefully supervised by an exemplary pastor especially appointed to this task by the bishop.[26]

New Evangelization: The Deacon in the Third Christian Millennium

252.   "The vocation of the permanent deacon is a great gift of God to the Church and for this reason is 'an important enrichment for the Church's mission.'"[27] Being called and sent by the Lord have always been important, but in contemporary historical circumstances they acquire a particular urgency. "The mission of Christ the Redeemer, which is entrusted to the Church, is still very far from completion. . . . An overall view of the human race shows that this

mission is still only beginning and that we must commit ourselves wholeheartedly to its service."[28] To this end, the ministry of the deacon holds great promise, especially for the urgent missionary and pastoral work of the new evangelization. The post-ordination path in diaconal formation should give priority to this task. Pope John Paul II stresses this urgency: "Heralds of the Gospel are needed who are experts in humanity, profoundly knowing the heart of contemporary man, who share his hopes and joys, his fears and sorrow and, at the same time, who are contemplatives in love with God."[29]

IV. Diocesan Organization for Post-Ordination Path Formation

A Diocesan Post-Ordination Program
253.   With the approval of the diocesan bishop, a program for the ongoing formation of deacons should be designed annually. It must take into consideration the demands made upon the deacons by their pastoral ministry, distances to be traveled, the frequency of gatherings, their time commitments to their families and secular employment, as well as the differing ages and needs of the deacons. In some places, regional or interdiocesan collaboration should be given serious consideration.[30] The use of distance-learning modules also should be explored, especially when travel is a hardship.[31]

Diocesan Policy
254.   Each diocesan Church is to establish a basic minimum of continuing education hours to be fulfilled on an annual basis by all diocesan deacons in active service.[32] This would be in addition to time allocated for the annual diaconal community retreat.

Models for Post-Ordination Formation
255.   At times, the post-ordination path in diaconal formation may be accomplished in common with priests, religious, and laity of the diocese to enhance collaborative ministerial formation in the diocese. This would use the resources of the diocese in a prudent manner.[33] However, sensitivity to the timing of such events is important, especially for deacons who are engaged in secular employment. On other occasions, ongoing formation programs should be specifically designed for deacons and particularly address the threefold ministry of word, liturgy, and charity.

256.   The models presented earlier in aspirant and candidate formation all lend themselves to a post-ordination formation methodology. Some additional possibilities might include the following:

a.   Diocesan, regional, or national conferences
b.   Workshops and seminars
c.   Educational and developmental themes for retreats and days of recollection
d.   Self-guided study
e.   Distance learning
f.   Ministry reflection groups
g.   Mentoring groups among deacons that meet to discuss ministry, exchange experiences, advance formation, and encourage each other in fidelity

NORMS

1.   A program should be planned for the first three years of their diaconal ministry. They should be supervised by a pastor appointed to this ministry by the diocesan bishop. The program should be coordinated by the director for deacon personnel. (251)
2.   Each diocesan Church should establish a basic minimum of continuing education hours to be fulfilled on an annual basis by all diocesan deacons in active service. (254)

NOTES

1   DMLPD, no. 65.

2   Ibid., no. 71, 63.

3   Ibid., no. 68; cf. Footnote 204 of DMLPD, no. 68.

4   Ibid., no. 75.

5   1 Tm 4:14-16.

6   DMLPD, no. 68.

7   Ibid., no. 76.

8   Ibid., no. 81.

9   FP, p. 33.

10   DMLPD, no. 69.

11   Ibid., no. 70.

12   Ibid., no. 44, citing Second Vatican Council, Decree *Presbyterorum Ordinis*, no. 12a.

13   Ibid., no. 45.

14   Ibid., no. 60.

15   Ibid., no. 60; Mt. 26:41.

16   Ibid., no. 61.

17   PDV, no. 72.

18   DMLPD, no. 72; cf. also nos. 65 and 71.

19   Ibid., no. 67.

20   Ibid., no. 73.

21   Ibid.

22   Congregation for the Clergy, *Directory on the Ministry and Life of Priests* (January 31, 1994) (Washington, D.C.: United States Catholic Conference, 1994), no. 78. (This is analogous for diaconal formation.)

23   DMLPD, no. 39.

24   Ibid., no. 66.

25   Ibid., no. 77.

26   Ibid.

27   PDO, no. 2.

28   Pope John Paul II, Encyclical Letter, *On the Permanent Validity of the Church's Missionary Mandate* (*Redemptoris Missio*) (December 7, 1990) (Washington, D.C.: United States Catholic Conference, 1990), no. 1.

29   Pope John Paul II, Allocution to the Sixth Symposium of European Bishops (November 11, 1985).

30   DMLPD, no. 79.

31   Cf. this *Directory*, Chapter Eight, nos. 262-265, on distance learning.

32   Ibid., no. 76.

33   Ibid., no. 78.

CHAPTER EIGHT

ORGANIZATION, STRUCTURE, AND PERSONNEL FOR DIACONAL FORMATION

I. Organization

Diocesan Plan for Diaconal Ministry

257. The establishment or renewal of diaconal ministry within a diocesan Church needs to be conceived and established within an overall diocesan plan for ministry in which the diaconate is seen as an integral component in addressing pastoral needs. In this way, deacons, who are ordained for service to the diocesan Church, will have a richer and firmer sense of their identity and purpose, as will those who collaborate in ministry with them.

The importance of a diocesan plan for ministry

Resources for Organization

258. Primary resources to guide a diocese in its discernment and readiness for the reestablishment or renewal of the diaconate are the documents of the Holy See: *Basic Norms for the Formation of Permanent Deacons* and *Directory for the Ministry and Life of Permanent Deacons*, as well as this *National Directory for the Formation, Ministry, and Life of Permanent Deacons in the United States*. These resources establish norms and directives that each diocese is to follow in the formation, ministry, and life of their deacons. Those responsible for the planning and implementation of the diaconal program should be thoroughly familiar with the intent and content of these documents.

Primary resources for norms and directives

259. The Secretariat for the Diaconate of the United States Conference of Catholic Bishops is also at the service of the diocesan bishop, especially regarding procedures for planning, requesting review of a formation proposal, and implementing the diaconate. Formal review of existing programs by a visiting team organized by the Bishops' Committee on the Diaconate is another resource available through the secretariat.

USCCB Secretariat for the Diaconate

II. Structures

Diocesan Program for Diaconal Formation

260.   "The diocese should provide appropriate structures for the formation,"[1] ministry, and life of deacons. Possible structures include an office, a policy board, admissions and evaluation committees, and so forth. Some practical functions of a diocesan diaconate structure include collaboration, formation planning, policy development, and post-ordination activities.[2]

Models for Diaconal Formation

261.   Various models for diaconal formation have developed in the United States. They provide the essential components for diaconal formation independently or in affiliation with other institutions.

1.   The **freestanding** structure is the most common model for diaconal formation in the United States. Within this diocesan structure, diaconal formation takes place in its entirety, usually with personnel drawn from the various academic, spiritual and formational resources of the diocese.

2.   The **college/university-**related model incorporates one or more parts of formation from diocesan staff and resources, while one or several parts of formation, such as the intellectual and/or pastoral, are provided and supervised by a Catholic college or university, usually located within the diocese. In these situations, diocesan coordinators carefully and comprehensively integrate the components of formation. Similar to the college/university model is the model that involves a **graduate school of theology**.

3.   A **diocesan or religious seminary** may offer valuable resources for the formation of deacons. The unique and dedicated role of the seminary for priestly formation and the distinction between priestly and diaconal identities must be maintained. "Prudent, limited" use of seminary facilities may be a useful resource available to the bishop in the formation of deacon candidates.[3]

4.   In a **collaborative** model, several specific groups, such as religious institutes or dioceses of a province, may choose to unite

their resources. Each group maintains separate formation directors and selection processes, but join together for one or more parts of formation. Care should be taken to ensure that the various components of formation are integrated in a comprehensive manner so that each participating group has a clear understanding of its specific responsibilities.

Distance Learning

262.   Regional provinces, as well as large individual dioceses, may consider employing distance learning as an alternative model for achieving part of the intellectual and pastoral dimensions of diaconal formation. The flexibility that distance learning offers can be a desirable feature in diaconal formation, as it honors a family life perspective in formation and ministry and recognizes the multiple demands on the participants that can make it difficult to be present at one location.[4]

263.   In the United States, a significant number of educational institutions, such as a local community colleges or universities, have the capacity to conduct video interactive conferencing with multiple sites in a state, county, and city. This technology provides one format for distance learning and is usually available to organizations and institutions as a public service. Some dioceses in the United States make good use of this technology.

264.   Another rapidly developing distance-learning format is the online seminar. Through the accessibility of the World Wide Web, Internet seminars and courses in theological, pastoral, and religious studies are being expanded at a reasonable cost to the participant. These courses are offered on undergraduate, graduate, and adult extension levels through Catholic colleges and universities in the United States and throughout the world. If a distance-learning format is incorporated into the diocesan program for part of the intellectual and pastoral dimensions in formation, it is the responsibility of the diocesan bishop to verify that the course of study offered fulfills the requirements of the *Basic Norms for the Formation of Permanent Deacons,* the *Directory for the Ministry and Life of Permanent Deacons,* and this *Directory.* The course must be complete, be in harmony with magisterial teaching, and be taught by a competent instructor. Of particular interest in distance learning is

Distance learning

Verification of the course of study

the availability on the Internet of major theological libraries and research centers throughout the world. A valuable resource in this regard is the web site of the Congregation for the Clergy, *www.clerus.org.*[5]

265.   Distance learning alone cannot build a diaconal formation community. However, it is a powerful instrument that supports a family perspective in diaconal formation, as well as an adult's capacity for self-formation with professional guidance.

III. The Role of the Diocesan Bishop in Diaconate Formation

The bishop:
Primary formator

266.   In the formation of deacons, "the first *sign and instrument* of the Spirit of Christ is the proper Bishop. . . . He is the one ultimately responsible for the discernment and formation" of aspirants and candidates, as well as the pastoral care of deacons.[6] He discharges this responsibility personally, as well as through "suitable associates" who assist him—the director of deacon formation and the director of deacon personnel. Both directors are accountable directly to the bishop or, in his absence, to a priest whom the bishop has appointed as his delegate: e.g., vicar general, vicar for clergy.[7] While the bishop may exercise his responsibility through his formation associates, nevertheless "he will commit himself, as far as is possible, to knowing personally those who are preparing for the diaconate."[8]

IV. Recruitment and Preparation of Formation Personnel

Competent staffing

267.   Because of the specialized nature of deacon formation and in order to ensure continuity among program personnel, the diocesan bishop or religious ordinary should encourage experienced and qualified priests and deacons to consider preparing themselves for the apostolate of deacon formation. Religious and lay persons may assist in suitable capacities in deacon formation; those selected by the bishop to do so should receive appropriate preparation for their role.

Continuity

Climate of stability

268.   Continuity in staffing and programming, as well as a planned transition in personnel, ought to receive the highest priority. The

administrative staff and formation faculty should comply with the personnel policies established by the diocesan Church for its clergy and lay staff, policies that may include term limits. Such compliance will help in planning for an orderly transition among formation personnel.

269.   Opportunities for sabbaticals, training, and internships for priests, deacons, and professional lay employees in preparation for eventual placements on the diaconal formation staff should be anticipated and scheduled as far in advance as possible.

V. Aspirant/Candidate Formation Personnel

270.   For the administration of the aspirant and candidate paths in diaconate formation, the following personnel have a special responsibility.

Director of Formation

271.   The director of formation, who should be either a priest or a deacon,[9] is appointed by the diocesan bishop to be head of the deacon formation program. He reports directly to the bishop and should have regular communication with him. The director is ultimately responsible for both aspirant and candidate formation. However, the number of participants in either path may require the additional appointment of an associate. The director oversees the implementation of the formation program. He conducts regularly scheduled assessments; makes home and parish visitations; supervises the formation team, faculty, and mentors; and maintains contact with the aspirants' and candidates' pastors.

Responsibilities of the formation director

272.   The director should be familiar with the diaconate—its history, theology, and practice. He should have parish experience, as well as practical skills and experience in formation, curriculum development, adult educational methodology, vocational discernment, supervision, and administration. He should be capable of providing spiritual leadership to the formation community. In most dioceses, the director of formation fulfills several administrative functions, except the spiritual direction of aspirants and candidates.[10]

Qualities of an effective director

Director of Spiritual Formation[11]

273.   The director of spiritual formation assists the director of formation by coordinating the entire spiritual formation program, giving

Responsibilities of the director of spiritual formation

it unity and direction. He makes provision for the individual spiritual direction of each aspirant and candidate. He also may serve as a spiritual director for an aspirant and/or candidate. He provides an orientation to the spiritual dimension in aspirant and candidate formation to other priest spiritual directors, who have been chosen by the aspirants or candidates with the approval of the bishop.[12] The director of spiritual formation provides for the liturgical life and prayer of the aspirant and candidate communities, making appropriate provision for the celebration of the Eucharist, the Liturgy of the Hours, and opportunities for celebration of the sacrament of penance in formation gatherings. He is also responsible for retreats and days of recollection, assuring that they are well planned and carefully executed. The director of spiritual formation, who must be a priest,[13] is nominated by the director of formation and approved and appointed by the bishop.

Qualifications of the director of spiritual formation

274.   The director of spiritual formation must be dedicated to the Church's *diakonia* and particularly knowledgeable of the diaconate and its mission within the Church. He should possess formal training in spirituality and related areas, including ascetical and spiritual theology, pastoral counseling, and referral skills.

Coordinator of Pastoral Field Education

Responsibilities of the coordinator of pastoral field education

275.   An integral formation must relate the human, spiritual, and intellectual dimensions to pastoral practice. "The whole formation imparted [to aspirants and candidates for the diaconate] . . . aims at preparing them to enter into communion with the charity of Christ. . . . Hence their formation in its different aspects must have a fundamentally pastoral character."[14] To ensure that all pastoral field education experiences are closely integrated with the human, spiritual, and intellectual dimensions of formation, the coordinator of pastoral field education assists the director of formation in the apostolic formation of aspirants and candidates. He systematically introduces the aspirants and candidates into suitable pastoral experiences, equipping them with practical skills for pastoral and, eventual, diaconal ministry. The coordinator for pastoral field formation, who must be either a priest or a deacon, is nominated by the director of formation and is approved and appointed by the bishop. The coordinator for pastoral field formation corresponds to the office of the "pastor (or other minister)" required by the *Basic Norms for the*

Formation of Permanent Deacons of the Congregation for Catholic Education. He administers and coordinates the program of field education for the aspirant and candidate paths of formation. In consultation with the director of formation and others responsible for formation, he arranges for the pastoral field placement of each participant, including an orientation and training of those who assist him in the field placement. Supervisory skills cannot be presumed, and teaching them is a high priority. Good supervision guarantees that the pastoral field experience remains systematically educative and formational. The coordinator for pastoral field formation also provides a written assessment of the participant's pastoral field education experience. The coordinator for pastoral field formation has faculty status, thereby ensuring that all pastoral field experiences are carefully coordinated with the other dimensions in formation.

276.   It is important that the coordinator for pastoral field formation have parish experience, be familiar with pastoral education, be knowledgeable in theology and supervisory techniques, be familiar with the value and practice of theological reflection—its goals, objectives, and methods. He should possess formal training in supervision and counseling. Since the pastoral service of the diocesan Church extends to all individuals and groups, including all social classes, with special concern for the poor and those alienated from society, the coordinator for pastoral field formation also should have knowledge of the needs and resources within the diocesan Church and be familiar with deacon placements within the diocese and their effectiveness in the local Church.

Qualifications of the coordinator for pastoral formation

Faculty

SELECTION

277.   Faculty members are nominated by the director of formation and approved and appointed by the bishop. The faculty contributes in a significant way to the formation of future deacons. The quality and expertise of the faculty determine the qualities and abilities of the future deacon. The Congregation for Catholic Education has formulated, in its *Directives Concerning the Preparation of Seminary Educators*, specific criteria to guide the selection of faculty that apply to the selection of diaconal faculty members as well.[15] The criteria established by the Congregation are highlighted in the notes of this chapter.[16]

Vatican directives for educators

EXPECTATIONS

278.   Each member of the faculty is expected to do the following:

a.   Submit a course outline and list of required textbooks[17]
b.   Participate in the assessment of aspirants or candidates for their continuance in the formation process and eventual readiness for ordination to the diaconate
c.   Be available for student consultation, providing feedback to them on their achievements as well as further development needed
d.   Submit a written assessment of the student's level of achievement in the course, as well as any area that may require further growth
e.   Participate whenever possible in the formation community's life and prayer, faculty discussions, and in-service programming
f.   Be familiar with and experienced in adult learning processes and a family perspective in class preparation, presentation, and assignment

279.   The faculty should expect assistance from the director of formation in the following areas:

a.   An **orientation** to
    i.   The dimension in diaconal formation: the formation process, including philosophy, mission, formation goals, and doctrinal understanding of the identity and mission of deacons
    ii.   The personal, ministerial, and academic background of current aspirants, candidates, and deacons
b.   **In-service programming** that includes the following:
    i.   Vatican documents on deacon formation, such as *Basic Norms for the Formation of Permanent Deacons* and *Directory for the Ministry and Life of Permanent Deacons*; the *Instruction on Certain Questions Regarding the Collaboration of the Non-Ordained Faithful in the Sacred Ministry of Priests*
    ii.   *National Directory for the Formation, Ministry, and Life of Permanent Deacons in the United States*
    iii.   The role of field education in the academic curriculum and assessment
c.   **Equitable compensation/stipend** based on travel to and from the formation site, course preparation and grading, and participation in evaluation sessions and faculty meetings, student conferences, and in-service programming. The basic criteria to be used

in determining a just stipend are the level of a faculty member's academic credentials and experience, together with the time commitment in preparing, teaching, and counseling participants

d. An **educational environment** that includes proper equipment, classroom space, and materials

e. **Feedback** from the administrators and students regarding the faculty member's presentations and response

f. A **formal service agreement** between the director of formation and the individual faculty member that incorporates the above expectations and that makes as explicit as possible mutual services and obligations

Service agreement

Mentors

280. The director of formation, with the approval and appointment of the bishop, should designate mentors from among deacons or priests who are knowledgeable and competent to assist him in assessing the potential and qualifications of those in formation. The mentor is equivalent to the "tutor" described in the *Basic Norms for the Formation of Permanent Deacons*. The mentor is charged with following the formation of those committed to his care, offering support and encouragement. Depending upon the size of the formation community, a mentor will be responsible for one aspirant or candidate, or he may be invited to minister to a small group of aspirants or candidates. Mentors receive their orientation and supervision from the director of formation. They also help the director for pastoral formation facilitate theological reflection among those assigned to them. Mentors are members of the formation team and are invited "to collaborate with the director of formation in the programming of the different formational activities and in the preparation of the judgment of suitability."[18]

VI. Advisory Structures for Aspirant and Candidate Paths of Formation

281. Members of advisory structures should be representative of the pastors, deacons, deacons' wives, religious, and laity. Whenever possible they ought to reflect the variety of cultures and diverse ethnic and racial groups in the diocese. Members may be nominated by the director of formation and be approved and appointed by the bishop. The director of formation serves as an *ex officio*, non-voting member.

Diocesan support structures for the formation program

282.   Some possible advisory structures include the following.

Formation Policy Board

283.   The bishop may constitute a formation policy board to assist him and the director of formation in matters of formation. The functions of this board are to advise on the planning, implementation, and evaluation of the formation program. Practical skills and experience in curriculum development, formation work, discernment and supervision, spiritual direction, counseling, finances, planning, and organizational development would be some of the essential criteria in selecting appropriate board members. The board might also be set up in such a way that not all the members' specific terms of service conclude together, allowing for continuity in the board's deliberations. The membership and procedures of the board should be determined in accordance with its statutes, as approved by the bishop.

Committee on Admission and Scrutinies

284.   As prescribed by the Congregation for Divine Worship and the Discipline of the Sacraments, the diocesan bishop is to establish a committee on admission and scrutinies, unless another structure exists. The formation policy board might include this responsibility among its tasks. The committee on admission and scrutinies could, thereby, be constituted as a subcommittee of the formation policy board with its members selected from the board. The specific responsibilities of this committee are to review and recommend applicants for admission to aspirant and candidate formation, nominate aspirants for the Rite of Admission to Candidacy, and review and nominate candidates for installation into the ministries of lector and acolyte, and eventually, for ordination to the diaconate.[19]

VII. Post-Ordination Formation Personnel

Pastoral care of deacons and the diaconal community

285.   It is a particular responsibility of the bishop to provide for the pastoral care of the deacons and the diaconal community in his diocese. This care is discharged both personally and through the director of deacon personnel. Special care should always be shown to those deacons experiencing difficulties because of personal circumstances. Whenever possible the bishop should attend the deacons' community meetings, as well as those of the deacon community

board or the deacon personnel board, if these structures have been authorized and constituted. If the bishop is unable to attend, he may designate a priest—e.g., his vicar general or vicar for the clergy—to represent him in his absence.[20]

The Director of Deacon Personnel

286.   The diocesan bishop appoints the director of deacon personnel. He is directly responsible to the bishop. The director, who is to be either a priest or a deacon, should have regular and comprehensive communications with the bishop on matters regarding individual deacons, as well as their families.[21] In fulfilling his responsibilities, the director of deacon personnel should be thoroughly familiar with the intent and context of the *Directory for the Ministry and Life of Permanent Deacons* of the Congregation for the Clergy, and this *Directory*, especially the post-ordination components.

Director of deacon personnel

287.   The director serves as the bishop's representative in the implementation of the post-ordination path in diaconate formation. He assists the bishop in his supervision of the spiritual and personal welfare of deacons and their families. The duties of the director of deacon personnel, although separate, parallel those of the director of formation. He is not, however, responsible for those in aspirant and candidate formation.[22]

Formation and post-ordination administration should be distinct

288.   In most dioceses, the director of deacon personnel fulfills several administrative functions, except that of the spiritual direction of deacons.[23] The director of deacon personnel, together with the deacon's designated pastor or priest supervisor (if the deacon is assigned to an office or agency not directed by a priest), as well as a representative of that office or agency, and the deacon are to be involved in the preparation of the text of the bishop's *decree of appointment*. Further, the director oversees the program for the newly ordained. He also ministers, as delegated by the bishop, to the other deacons in their assigned ministries, conducting regularly scheduled visits with the deacons and their families, reviewing and evaluating diaconal assignments, and making appropriate recommendations to the bishop. He assists the bishop and the deacons' designated pastors in planning and implementing an annual program for diaconate continuing formation. He further assists the bishop and the designated pastors in their pastoral care of deacons

Responsibilities for the director of deacon personnel

and their families, especially monitoring those living and ministering outside the diocese, or deacons who may be ill or on a ministerial leave of absence. The director of deacon personnel also complements the bishop's presence to and care for retired deacons and their families, as well as to deacon widowers and widows and their families.

289.   At the discretion of the diocesan bishop, the director of deacon personnel may be appointed as a liaison to diocesan departments and public agencies, as well as parishes, on diaconal matters.

VIII. Post-Ordination Advisory Structures

Deacon Community Board

290.   The bishop may constitute a deacon community board to represent the deacons and their spouses. Members of such an organization would include a suitable number of deacons and wives elected by the diaconal community and others appointed by the bishop, in accordance with the organization's statutes, as approved by the ordinary. The statutes should govern everything that relates to the purposes and operation of the organization. A responsibility of the community board could be the preparation of a deacon personnel handbook, specifying appropriate norms or policies—rights, obligations, and responsibilities—for deacons serving the diocesan Church. The bishop must authorize this text. This board also could assist the bishop in planning, coordinating, and evaluating the post-ordination educational and spiritual formation program. The bishop or a priest designated as the bishop's delegate in his absence serves as the board's president.[24]

Deacon Personnel Board

291.   It may be desirable for the diocesan bishop to establish a deacon personnel board to assist him in assigning and evaluating deacons. Its role would be analogous to that of the priests' personnel board, which assists the diocesan bishop in ascertaining appropriate and suitable assignments based on the needs of the particular Church and the capabilities of the individual. The establishment of a deacon personnel board could be a valuable resource to the bishop and director of deacon personnel. If constituted, the bishop or, in his absence, a priest designated by the bishop (e.g., his vicar general, vicar for the clergy) chairs this board. This board should maintain

appropriate links to other diocesan entities to ensure a collaborative and integrative approach to the understanding and use of deacons and diaconal ministry throughout the diocese.

NORMS

1. The diocesan bishop is the one ultimately responsible for the discernment and formation of aspirants and candidates, as well as the pastoral care of deacons. He exercises his responsibility personally, as well as through his director of diaconal formation and the director of deacon personnel whom he has appointed and who are responsible directly to him or, in his absence, to a priest whom he has appointed as his delegate. (267)

2. The director of formation, who must be either a priest or a deacon, is appointed by the diocesan bishop to be head of the diaconate office. He is directly responsible to the bishop. (272)

3. The bishop may set up a formation policy board to assist him and the director of formation in matters of diaconal formation. (283)

4. The director of spiritual formation, who must be a priest, is nominated by the director of formation. He is approved and appointed by the bishop. He personally oversees the spiritual formation of each participant and provides an orientation to other spiritual directors, who must also be priests and who may be chosen by the aspirants or candidates with the approval of the bishop. (274)

5. The coordinator for pastoral formation, who corresponds to "the pastor (or other minister)" required by the *Basic Norms for the Formation of Permanent Deacons* of the Congregation for Catholic Education, is nominated by the director of formation.[25] He is approved and appointed by the bishop. (276)

6. Faculty members are nominated by the director of formation and then approved and appointed by the bishop. (278)

7. Mentors for aspirants and candidates, who are to be knowledgeable and competent to assist the director of formation, are nominated from among priests and deacons by the director of formation. They also are approved and appointed by the bishop. Mentors are charged with closely following the formation of those committed to their care, offering support and encouragement. (281)

8. If a distance-learning model is incorporated into the diocesan formation program, it is the responsibility of the diocesan bishop to verify that the course of study offered fulfills the requirements of this *Directory*. It must be complete, be in harmony with magisterial teaching, and be taught by a competent instructor. (265)

9. The diocesan bishop should appoint a director of deacon personnel, who should be either a priest or a deacon. At the discretion of the diocesan bishop, the director of deacon personnel serves as the bishop's representative in directing the post-ordination path of formation and assists the bishop in the supervision of diocesan deacons. This director also coordinates the program for the newly ordained deacons. (286-289)

NOTES

1   PDG (1984), no. 52.

2   Some of the specific responsibilities would include the following:

Collaboration

i   Involvement of and accountability to the diocesan bishop

ii   Relationship with diocesan offices, departments, and agencies; linkage with other ministry preparation programs in the diocese

iii Liaison with pastors, priests, religious, and laity

iv   Relationship with regional and national diaconate associations and organizations

Planning

i   Appointment, readiness, and supervision of appropriate personnel to carry out the diaconal formation plan/activities

ii   Initial and ongoing catechesis of the diaconate

iii Integrate diaconal ministry into the local Church

Policy Development

i   Development of policies and procedures for recruitment, screening, and admissions

ii   Development of policies and procedures for evaluation of those in formation

iii Development of the program, taking account of concrete needs and local circumstances

Post-Ordination Activities

i   Development of policies and procedures for diocesan diaconal life

ii   Support structures for deacons, deacon spouses, and families

iii Policies/procedures for assignment and review of deacons

iv   Continuing formation and spiritual formation policies and program opportunities

v   Regular assessment of diaconal ministry in the diocese

3   Congregation for Catholic Education and the Congregation for the Clergy, *Joint Study of the U.S. Draft Document—National Directory for the Formation, Ministry and Life of Permanent Deacons in the United States*, Prot. No. 78/2000 (March 4, 2002).

4   Cf. Congregation for the Clergy, *General Directory for Catechesis* (August 15, 1998) (Washington, D.C.: United States Conference of Catholic Bishops-Libreria Editrice Vaticana, 1998), no. 160.

5   The Congregation for the Clergy offers its web site to assist in the continuing formation of priests, deacons, and catechists. The web site provides a library on the magisterial teachings of the Sovereign Pontiffs, with recent documentation from the Holy Father, Church Fathers, Sacred Writings; it provides links to several theological libraries; live teleconferences or documentation from the teleconferences on Christology, Ecclesiology, Sacramental and Moral Theology, Mariology, Pneumatology; Statistical information on diocesan, religious priests, and deacons; as well as an e-mail option for updated information on future offerings.

6   BNFPD, no. 19.

7   Ibid., no. 16; cf. also nos. 21, 42, 44, 62; cf. DMLPD, nos. 3, 78, 80.

8   Ibid., no. 19.

9   Ibid., no. 21.

10   Ibid.

11   Ibid., no. 23.

12   PDV, no. 57; cf. BNFPD, no. 85.

13   "It is the intention of our Dicasteries that the variety of offices in diaconal formation and post-ordination ministry: the Director of the Formation Program, the Coordinator for Pastoral Formation, Mentors, the Director of Deacon Personnel should be reserved to clerics —and in the case of the Director of Spiritual Formation (an office not mentioned in the *Ratio fundamentalis*), Pastors and Priest Pastoral Supervisors, they must be a priest." Congregation for Catholic Education and the Congregation for the Clergy, *Joint Study of the US Draft Document—National Directory for the Formation, Ministry and Life of Permanent Deacons in the United States*, Prot. No. 78/2000 (March 4, 2002).

14   Ibid., no. 24.

15   Congregation for Catholic Education, *Directives Concerning the Preparation of Seminary Educators* (November 4, 1993) (Washington, D.C.: United States Catholic Conference, 1994), pp. 5-6.

16   The following considerations are this *Directory's* commentaries on the criteria for faculty selections as established by the Congregation for Catholic Education:

    i   A *spirit of faith*: A lived commitment to the Church, its Magisterium, and the deposit of faith accompanied and sustained by a love of prayer—the educator who lives by faith teaches more by what he is than by what he says

    ii   A *pastoral sense*: A commitment to the pastoral-theological vision of the Second Vatican Council and to the identity and mission of diaconal ministry that the council and post-conciliar documents promote in the contemporary Church; a sensitivity also from their own participation in the pastoral charity of Christ

    iii   A *spirit of communion*: Collaboration and understanding of their role in the vocational discernment for admission to candidacy and ordination to the diaconate

    iv   *Human maturity and psychological equilibrium*: A right consciousness of oneself, of one's own values and limits, honestly recognized and accepted

    v   A *clear and mature capacity to love*: An ability to be an example and model of the primacy of love in service—a capacity and inclination to self-giving attention to the other person, to an understanding of his concerns, and to a clear perception of his real good

    vi   *Listening, dialogue, and the capacity for communication*: The success of the formational relationship depends in great part on these three capacities

    vii   *Positive and critical attention to modern culture*: Inspired by the cultural richness of Christianity (i.e., rooted in biblical, liturgical, and patristic sources), a broad knowledge of contemporary culture—a positive and critical awareness of the transmission of contemporary culture, making it easier to enable students to form an interior synthesis in the light of faith.

Following are some additional criteria:

i   *Academic qualifications*: An advanced degree in theology, religious studies, or a related field; a demonstrated ability as a competent teacher

ii   *Multicultural sensitivity*: Experience with multicultural, gender, economic, and educational diversity

iii   *Adult formation*: Ability to teach adults in theory and practice; knowledge and experience in adult developmental theory and methodologies

iv   *Diversity*: Represent the ethnicity, racial, and cultural diversity of the diocesan Church

v   *Knowledge and experience of the diaconate*: Knowledge of the identity and ministry of deacons in the Church

17   Regarding the selection of textbooks, faculty presenters should be familiar with the USCCB's *Guidelines for Doctrinally Sound Catechetical Materials* (Washington, D.C.: United States Catholic Conference, 1990). The following excerpts from that document are provided here for easier accessibility to several highlights of the text:

The first principle of doctrinal soundness is that the Christian message be *authentic* and *complete*. For expressions of faith and moral teachings to be authentic, they must be in harmony with the doctrine and traditions of the Catholic Church, which are safeguarded by the bishops who teach with a unique authority. For completeness, the message of salvation, which is made up of several parts that are closely interrelated, must, in due course, be presented in its entirety, with an eye to leading individuals and communities to maturity of faith. Completeness also implies that individual parts be presented in a balanced way, according to the capacity of the learners and in the context of a particular doctrine. (p. 7)

The second principle in determining the doctrinal soundness of catechetical materials is the recognition that the mystery of faith is *incarnate* and *dynamic* [and that the discourse of faith with adults must take serious account of their experience, of their conditioning, and of the challenges which they encounter in life]. The mystery of the divine plan for human salvation, revealed in the person of Jesus Christ and made known in the Sacred Scriptures, continues as a dynamic force in the world through the power of the Holy Spirit until finally all things are made subject to Christ and the kingdom is handed over to the Father "so that God may be all in all" (1 Cor 15:28). God's creative power is mediated in the concrete experiences of life, in personal development, in human relationships, in culture, in social life, in science and technology, and in "signs of the times." The *National Catechetical Directory* refers to the Scriptures, the teaching life and witness of the Church, the Church's liturgical life, and life experiences of various kinds as "signs of God's saving activity" in the world (NCD [*Sharing the Light of Faith: National Catechetical Directory for Catholics in the United States* (1979)], 42). These biblical, ecclesial, liturgical, and natural signs should inform the content and spirit of all catechetical materials. (p. 7)

A second set of guidelines—no less important than the first if catechesis is to be effective—are based on pastoral principles and practical concerns. They are reminders that catechetical materials must take into account the community for whom they are intended, the conditions in which they live, and the ways in which they learn (cf. GCD [*General Catechetical Directory* (1971)], Foreword). . . . Catechetical materials [must] take into consideration the needs of the Hispanic community and other ethnic and culturally diverse groups that comprise the Church in the United States. No single text or program can address the many cultures and groups that make up society in the United States, but all catechetical materials must take this diversity into account. Effective catechesis, as we have noted above, requires that the Church's teaching be presented correctly and in its entirety, and it is equally important to present it in ways that are attractive, appealing, and understandable by the individuals and communities to whom it is directed. (p. 23)

18   BNFPD, no. 22.

19   CL, Enclosure III.

20   DMLPD, no. 80.

21   Cf. BNFPD, no. 21: "could be either a priest or a deacon" is applied equivalently in this *Directory* to that of the director of deacon personnel. Cf., also, footnote no. 12, above.

22   Ibid.

23   Ibid.

24   DMLPD, no. 80.

25   BNFPD, no. 24.

CONCLUSION

292.   It is the desire of the United States Conference of Catholic Bishops that, as implemented in accord with local or regional resources, this *Directory* will provide a sure directive for promoting harmony and unity in diaconal formation and ministry throughout the United States and its territorial sees. In so doing, this *Directory* will ensure a certain uniformity in the identity, selection, and formation of deacons, as well as provide for more clearly defined pastoral objectives in diaconal ministries.

293.   This *Directory* is presented to the diaconal communities in the United States as a tangible expression of the Conference's gratitude to them for their dedicated ministry to God's People. It is also intended to challenge and encourage them to be, with greater dedication and clarity, the sacrament of Jesus—the Servant Christ to a servant Church.

APPENDIX I

SPECIFIC NORMATIVE ELEMENTS IN DIACONAL FORMATION

I. Introduction

294.   This section has been added to highlight the specific normative elements that ought to be part of the planning, implementation, and evaluation of a diaconal program. They need to be interpreted within the intent and context of this *Directory*.

II. Specific Normative Elements to Include in a Proposal for Review

295.   When a bishop submits a proposal to the Bishops' Committee on the Diaconate for review, he should provide descriptive information on the following normative elements for the formation, ministry, and life of deacons:

- The diocesan pastoral plan clarifying the deacon's identity, role, and participation in diocesan pastoral ministry
- The catechesis on the diaconate, covering content and process for its clergy, religious and lay staff, and the lay faithful of the diocese
- The organization and structures established within the diocese
- The academic/professional competencies, including the names and background of the administration, primary faculty, mentors, and other formation personnel selected to plan and implement the program, as well as the orientation program for the staff to the diaconate and diaconal formation
- The recruitment process, a collaborative activity of the departments for vocations, diaconal formation, and parochial pastors
- The recruitment processes to be employed in inviting applicants from communities reflecting the ethnic, racial, and cultural diversity of the diocese, including a copy of recruiting guidelines, materials, and application forms

- The screening procedures, particularly the psychological and personality testing that may be used—a list of the instruments, how they will be interpreted, and by whom
- The selection process, including the advisory structures that will make recommendations to the bishop, particularly the committee on admission and scrutinies, with its proposed composition and charter, if available
- The incorporation of the human, spiritual, intellectual, and pastoral dimensions of each path in diaconal formation; the engagement of participants in the pastoral ministries of the diocese and specific parishes
- The aspirant path in formation, specifying program length, formation contact hours, general content, the model of formation chosen, linkage with other diocesan formation programs (if any), assessment procedures, a list of those who will guide this path in formation and their professional competencies, and the aspirant's handbook (if available)
- The candidate path in formation, specifying program length, formation contact hours, course descriptions and methodology in compliance with the directives specified in the *Basic Norms for the Formation of Permanent Deacons* and this *Directory*, a list of the faculty and their academic/professional competencies, the model(s) chosen for formation, assessment procedures, a list of prescribed textbooks, and the candidate's handbook (if available)
- A declaration from the bishop regarding the verification of courses of study obtained through distance learning or Internet seminars
- The program for spiritual formation in each path in formation; the name and competencies of the spiritual director
- The level and content of the involvement of wives and families in the formation program, including any requirement policy for wives' participation
- The deacon personnel director and his competencies; the structures envisioned for the post-ordination path in formation; the provisions for the pastoral care of deacons in their ministry and life after ordination; the program for the newly ordained; supervision and review of the decree of appointment; assessment procedures; continuing spiritual, intellectual, and pastoral formation, as well as personalized training; ongoing formation

programming for wives and families; special care for deacons who are ill, widowed, and retired, and also for widows of deacons; inclusion of deacons within diocesan structures

- A description of the application of particular law governing deacons, as approved by the United States Conference of Catholic Bishops and applied within the diocese
- A copy of the deacon personnel policy handbook, with policies and procedures governing post-ordination diaconal ministry and life (if available)
- Plans for a regularly scheduled assessment of the formation program
- Procedures employed for maintaining a list of deacons with their ministerial assignments; pastoral care of retired or widowed deacons, as well as those living outside of the diocese

APPENDIX II

THE UNITED STATES CONFERENCE OF CATHOLIC BISHOPS' COMMITTEE ON THE DIACONATE

I. Responsibilities

296. In November 1968, the Bishops' Committee on the Diaconate was formally constituted by the National Conference of Catholic Bishops. Its principal functions are to

- Provide diocesan bishops with information concerning diaconal formation, ministry, and life; the Ordinary is encouraged to consult with the Committee for its review of the diocesan formation structures and staffing, content, and ministerial practices prior to a diocese's implementation of the permanent diaconate
- Establish national norms for the selection, formation, placement, ministry, and life of aspirants, candidates, and deacons
- Provide, at the request of local ordinaries, a formal evaluation of diaconal formation and ministry after they have been implemented
- Initiate a series of monographs as part of a structured catechesis on the diaconate
- Initiate and supervise national studies of the diaconate in the United States, as requested by the Conference
- Maintain an updated statistical database on deacons in the United States

Accountability and support

II. The Bishops' Committee and National Diaconate Associations

297. With the growth of the diaconate in the United States, various groupings of deacons and others associated in diaconate formation and ministry have formed national associations to foster a collaborative relationship among their members. At the invitation of the Bishops' Committee for the Diaconate, the executive officers of these associations serve as advisors to the committee. This affiliation promotes the accountability of each association to the committee.1 In addition, these associations bring a unique perspec-

Formal consultation

tive to the committee's deliberations by representing the diaconate in its rich diversity of cultures, races, ethnicities, and ministries. Their contribution to the work of the Committee is invaluable.

III. The Secretariat for the Diaconate

The United States Conference of Catholic Bishops has established a Secretariat for the Diaconate. The executive director of the secretariat serves the chairman and members of the committee. The executive director is also available to assist a diocesan bishop or religious ordinary with pre-ordination and post-ordination matters. An evaluation of a diocesan program by the Bishops' Committee on the Diaconate can be organized through the Secretariat for the Diaconate. This consultation would be helpful to a new diocesan bishop or could also occur every ten years in a currently active formation process.

NOTE

1　Cf. CIC, c. 278 §1 and §2; cf. also DMLPD, no. 11.

Index

SECONDARY DOCUMENT

BASIC STANDARDS
FOR READINESS

I. Model Standards for Readiness for Admission into the Aspirant Path

APPRECIATION/KNOWLEDGE OF	DEMONSTRATED ABILITY/SKILL
Human Dimension • His emotional, intellectual, physical, and personal limitations • A family perspective in his life	• To speak appropriately of his personal limitations and known boundaries with a sense of how these affect his life, family, employment, and present service ministry • To balance and prioritize his commitments to family, work, leisure, and ministry; to be self-disciplined
Spiritual Dimension • God's redeeming activity in his state of life, experience, and ministry • The importance of a both personal and communal prayer life	• To reflect/meditate in faith on his life with a sense of discovering God's will • To convey examples of God's presence in his life • To commit as a reader or extraordinary minister of the Eucharist; to serve his parish community, especially in charity and outreach to the needy; to be responsible and confident • To be both a leader and follower • To fulfill a commitment to a pattern of prayer; to participate frequently in the Eucharist and the Sacrament of Reconciliation; to participate in retreat experiences or a renewal group • To support others' growth in prayer; to show interest in sharing and serving with others

APPRECIATION/KNOWLEDGE OF	DEMONSTRATED ABILITY/SKILL

Intellectual Dimension

- The basic teachings of the Church

- To demonstrate familiarity with the *Catechism of the Catholic Church*

Pastoral Dimension

- Living the Gospel in his life, home, place of employment, and neighborhood

- To connect the teachings of the Church to daily living and his personal/communal (family, church, civic) responsibilities
- To be flexible in attitude and behavior; to be open to change; to analyze situations in light of the Gospel and the Church's teaching

Diaconal Vocation and Ministry

- A personal call to diaconal ministry with the Church and a sense of his capacity to commit himself to it in fidelity to his state in life and employment, with sufficient time for formation

- To witness to Gospel values in ways that are life-giving; to articulate his sense of a call to the diaconate primarily because of the needs of the Church, as well as for personal growth; and to articulate reasons that support his desire to be a deacon
- To be interested in and attracted to the diaconal *munera* of word, liturgy, and charity
- To be of service, beyond liturgical ministries, through church or civic involvement
- To support and encourage his pastor, as a representative for the parish community and staff
- To be docile to the presence of the Holy Spirit throughout the application and screening processes, acknowledging that ultimately it is the Church that verifies the call

II. Model Standards for Readiness for Admission into the Candidate Path

APPRECIATION/KNOWLEDGE OF	DEMONSTRATED ABILITY/SKILL

Human Dimension

- His personality (strengths and limitations), appropriate boundaries, and his talents and gifts; collaboration

- Models of faith and moral development through discussion and action

- The necessity for ongoing spiritual and academic development

- The role of respectful listening and tolerance in dialogue with others whose point of view may differ from his

- To be self-reflective; to reveal himself appropriately, sharing his experiences and attitudes with others as verified in the formation community, mentor group, pastoral ministry placement, and self-evaluation; to be both a leader and follower
- To use his knowledge to encourage others to reflect and share their experiences in dialogue and action
- To demonstrate the use of appropriate resources for his physical, emotional, and spiritual development; to take initiative in self-study and in completing home assignments
- To be a good listener, respect each person, and be accepted as a trusted participant who keeps confidences; to be open to change through reflective growth in understanding; to express his position candidly in sharing for study and dialogue, neither intimidating nor being intimidated in doing so
- To integrate and prioritize his personal boundaries relating to family, recreation, work, ministry, and time alone
- To contribute to and utilize a support system

APPRECIATION/KNOWLEDGE OF	DEMONSTRATED ABILITY/SKILL

Spiritual Dimension

- God's redeeming activity in his lifestyle, experiences, and ministries

- The *lectio divina* in the formation of a strong Christian spirituality

- His commitment to Christian ministry as rooted in the baptismal call

- A personal and communal prayer life

- His state in life, responsibilities, and role in diaconal discernment; diaconal celibacy and other commitments

- An ecumenical perspective in formation

- To reflect theologically on his faith experience through regular spiritual direction
- To pray the Scriptures, meditating on the mystery of God as our Father, Son, and Holy Spirit
- To foster an appreciation of baptismal ministry among others, enabling others to reflect upon their faith journey in relationship to this call
- To fulfill a regular commitment to a pattern of personal and communal prayer through frequent praying of the Liturgy of the Hours, especially morning and evening prayer; to participate frequently in the Eucharist and the Sacrament of Reconciliation, personal prayer and reading of the Bible, and devotion to Mary and to the saints; to plan and lead communal prayer
- To ascertain, if married, the quality of his relationship with his wife and children and the need for dialogue and mutual consent to continue in formation and move forward toward ordination; to make, if unmarried, a commitment to perpetual celibacy and live a single lifestyle in an appropriate manner
- To practice in prayer and action an attitude of discipleship to Christian unity, desiring to know more about other Christian denominations and other faith experiences and finding ways for mutual action in serving human needs

APPRECIATION/KNOWLEDGE OF	DEMONSTRATED ABILITY/SKILL

Intellectual Dimension

- The *Catechism of the Catholic Church*

- The Sacraments of Christian Initiation and the Sacrament of Holy Orders, especially the Order of Deacon

- The Eucharist as the summit and center of Christian communal life, especially in his formation community

- The Church's spiritual tradition, including its various paths of spirituality

- Pastoral resources

- To articulate the primary teachings of the Church and discuss contemporary issues in light of this teaching
- To speak informally on Christian vocations and ordained ministry, particularly the Order of Deacon and its threefold ministries of word, liturgy, and charity; to relate this knowledge to personal and communal vocation discernment
- To actively participate in the Eucharist as a lector or extraordinary minister of the Eucharist and in ministry to the sick
- To experience and invite others into meaningful expressions of prayer and forms of Christian spirituality
- To refer others to appropriate pastoral resources as needed

Pastoral Dimension

- Theological sources that ground, interpret, and guide the activity that constitutes the pastoral life of the Church

- Effective communication skills

- A multicultural perspective in formation; cultural communication patterns and their impact on goals and programming; resources for ethnic, racial, and cultural groups

- How to approach theological study from within the context of his pastoral experience and ministry

- To name appropriate theological resources useful to ministerial study and service
- To communicate effectively in spoken and written word
- To effectively use different cultural communication patterns whenever appropriate, and to use and guide others to appropriate multicultural resources
- To discern how God is calling him into ministry and to link, in reflection, his pastoral and personal experiences to theology— apprehending God's presence through touching the needs of the poor or afflicted; to be an advocate for people in need and a facilitator of the community's resources in response to human needs

APPRECIATION/KNOWLEDGE OF	DEMONSTRATED ABILITY/SKILL

Diaconal Vocation and Ministry

- His ongoing relationship with God as the source of his ministry and discernment of a diaconal vocation

- His call and his personal commitment to live the Good News in all aspects of life

- The role and ministry of the deacon within the faith community

- The teaching that it is the Church that calls and affirms the vocation to an ordained ministry

- To articulate his relationship with God and reasons for believing he has a call to the Order of Deacons within the formation community
- To articulate his call and commitment to his spiritual director and to the formation personnel and to communicate this through self/peer/formation/pastoral/ family assessments
- To articulate this understanding in ways that are life-giving and empowering within his family, place of employment, parish, formation community; to identify, call forth, affirm, and support the gifts, strengths, and talents of others
- To participate collaboratively in all aspects of formation; to be cooperative, open, and respectful to all who journey with him; to be receptive of insights offered by the formation personnel, his wife and family, peers, and pastor

III. Model Standards for Readiness for the Ordination and Post-Ordination Path

Appreciation/Knowledge of	Demonstrated Ability/Skill
Human Dimension 1. *Personal Qualities* • His gifts, personality, strengths and talents, and weaknesses and limitations and how they affect his ministry • His emotional, physical, and spiritual limitations • A family perspective and its impact on personal and ministerial activity • The complexities of daily life and ministry • The need for collaboration, reliability, accountability, and confidentiality • The use of imagination, enthusiasm, and humor • The influence and importance of peers in growing as deacon	• To engage in self-reflection and assess his abilities and limitations • To set healthy and responsible goals, maintain a healthy balance in his personal life and ministry, and develop positive support systems among family, friends, and peers • To infuse a family perspective into ministerial and personal scheduling and programming • To be flexible and assign appropriate priorities in varied circumstances • To demonstrate dependability and trustworthiness; to consult, plan, and support the pastoral team • To communicate with and relate to a wide variety of people • To participate in local, regional, and national professional associations; to promote and participate in diocesan programs, inservices, and community opportunities for deacon personnel

APPRECIATION/KNOWLEDGE OF	DEMONSTRATED ABILITY/SKILL

2. Relationship

- The various ministries, roles, and responsibilities of a deacon, especially in his relation to the pastor, parish staff, director of religious education, etc., as they relate to and serve the community

- The role and mission of the deacon in the universal, diocesan, and parochial communities

- Psycho-social dynamics and how cultural and ethnic differences affect ministerial practice

- The diversity of cultures and ethnic backgrounds within families and family systems; the role of culture in one's formation and self-awareness

- The dynamics of human growth and development

- Church structures at the arch/diocesan, regional, national and universal levels

- The role of the bishop, priests, and the pastor and their authority within the life of the diocese and parish

- To initiate, create, and sustain a positive, collaborative relationship with all colleagues in ministry; to discern, set, and maintain healthy and responsible boundaries in all pastoral relationships; to solicit input from those who will be affected by activities or policies

- To discern and evaluate ever-changing pastoral needs; to recruit, train, coordinate, and support parish volunteers in their ministerial and spiritual development; to find and use personal and professional support systems

- To recognize and work to dispel prejudices and cliques within his own life and that of the community; to network with others in challenging injustice

- To create and support viable structures and strategies for the inclusion of all families so they may participate actively in the planning and implementation of parish programs, including families of diverse cultural and ethnic backgrounds

- To create a hospitable environment where people are valued for who they are and who they might become; to conduct honest self-assessments and to help others to do the same

- To function appropriately at different levels of the diocesan Church while linking the parish structures and needs to larger church structures and resources

- To demonstrate appropriate respect, responsibility, and accountability to the bishop, pastor, or their delegates; to cooperate in the implementation of diocesan and parish policies and programs

Appreciation/Knowledge of	Demonstrated Ability/Skill
3. Personal Pastoral Care • Health: physical, psychological, and spiritual maintenance of himself as person and minister	• To establish appropriate health and spiritual boundaries to maintain personal health and care
• Sabbaticals, planned ministerial change in placement, and creativity in ministry discernment and placement; retirement; time off/vacations; a family perspective	• To demonstrate personal and professional preparedness in ministry; to use a ministry performance appraisal, needs assessment, and appropriate professional resources; to plan retirement; to spend time alone and with family and friends

Spiritual Dimension

Appreciation/Knowledge of	Demonstrated Ability/Skill
4. Spirituality and Prayer • The need for lifelong faith formation and education to grow as a person and a deacon	• To develop and commit to a plan for continuing personal and professional diaconal education and formation
• The response to the universal call to holiness with an integrated spirituality based on prayer, reflection, and liturgical participation in the Eucharist and Sacrament of Reconciliation	• To participate in the Eucharist daily or frequently; to participate regularly in reconciliation; to participate in ongoing spiritual formation (e.g., spiritual direction, retreats, community worship [especially the Liturgy of the Hours], personal prayer, meditation, visits to the Blessed Sacrament, personal penance and mortification, and devotion to Mary and the communion of saints
• Commitment to Christian ministry that builds on and expands one's baptismal call to ongoing personal conversion	
• Various spiritualities that have developed in the history and life of the Church	• To develop a lifelong commitment to leadership in Christian ministry, a driving force of the Church's service in the world
• The ways in which faith is active in his life and ministry	• To identify, affirm, and critique the various Christian spiritualities operative in himself and others; to discern new forms of prayer spiritualities in today's Church
• Moral and social issues as constitutive elements of a Gospel-based life	
• The value of receiving spiritual direction and personal counseling for his growth in wholeness	• To articulate his personal expression of faith with his spiritual director, formation team, faculty, pastor, colleagues, deacons, parishioners, etc.

APPRECIATION/KNOWLEDGE OF	DEMONSTRATED ABILITY/SKILL
• To integrate the wide spectrum of moral and human issues into his spiritual consciousness, prayer, and ministry: human rights, sexuality, economics, peace, ecology, moral ethics, solidarity with human needs, the preferential option for the poor • To maintain a commitment to regularly scheduled spiritual direction and to opportunities, as appropriate, for physical and psychological health in consultation with a professional advisor	

5. Spirituality and Marriage

• A commitment to the spiritual life in the context of his marriage and ministry • Relationship of marriage and ministry	• To communicate and share his ministry, prayer, and formation with wife and family; to demonstrate marital chastity in conformity to the magisterial teaching on marriage and sexuality • To balance marriage and ministry commitments

6. Spirituality and Celibacy

• A commitment to celibacy for the unmarried candidate and deacon • The potential for a celibate lifestyle for the married candidate and deacon	• To form a support system • To accept the gift of celibacy and be willing to accept it if so called; to speak truthfully about the gift and demands of a celibate life

APPRECIATION/KNOWLEDGE OF	DEMONSTRATED ABILITY/SKILL

Intellectual Dimension

7. Sacred Scripture

- The concepts of revelation, inspiration, historical development, and literary criticism

- The major themes and content of the Old and New Testaments

- Christian Scriptures, their stages of formation, and their place at the heart of Scriptures

- The power of Scripture to transform lives

- The major justice and peace themes in the Scriptures that root and foster Catholic social teaching

- The nature and skills for a successful transmission of Scripture in preaching

- The use of Scripture in theological reflection

- To articulate the foundational relationship of Scripture to the deposit of faith; to exercise appropriate exegetical skills in the context of church tradition and the needs of the community, especially in homiletic preparation
- To explain the major teachings found in the Scriptures to adults, teens, and children
- To interpret the Scriptures in harmony with the Magisterium and Catholic biblical scholarship
- To articulate the ways in which Scripture illumines and promotes his personal growth in faith and that of others
- To infuse justice and peace foundations and concerns in his preaching regularly and into all aspects of diaconal ministry
- To relate the Scriptures to his personal experience and that of others to transform and empower God's people

APPRECIATION/KNOWLEDGE OF	DEMONSTRATED ABILITY/SKILL
8. Theology of God, Christian Anthropology, and Christology	
• The relationship of philosophy and theology	• To demonstrate familiarity with John Paul II's *On the Relationship Between Faith and Reason*
• God as unity and trinity	• To explain the relationship of Trinitarian theology to Christology and ecclesiology
• God's self-revelation in creation, the person of Jesus, Scripture, liturgy, and people, especially the poor and needy	• To articulate and demonstrate reverence for this revelation and presence of God in the world through prayer, liturgy, ministries, and his present circumstances
• The basic aspects and principles of Christian anthropology: incarnation, grace, sin, redemption, resurrection, the sacredness of human life, etc.	• To identify and apply these basic principles to contemporary human issues; to be familiar with John Paul II's *The Gospel of Life*
• The sacredness and dignity of each human person	• To apply an appreciation of the sacredness and dignity of each human person to acts of charity and justice in hospitality and welcoming, direct pastoral care, ministry to migrants and immigrants, the ill, etc.; to advocate and organize for action
• Traditional and contemporary Christology: Jesus' historical life, mission, death, and resurrection	
• Eschatology: death, particular judgment, purgatory, hell, heaven, last judgment, and the hope of the new heaven and the new earth	• To articulate an understanding of the historical person and mission of Jesus; to engage in faith-sharing and reflection on Jesus' message as it impacts all aspects of human life
	• To articulate an understanding of the redemptive revelation of the kingdom, the hope of the resurrection, the second coming of Christ, and his own personal readiness in his ministry to those who are dying, viaticum, funeral liturgies, and counsel to families

Appreciation/Knowledge of	Demonstrated Ability/Skill
9. Ecclesiology • The Church's historical and traditional development and its relevance to the present Church; the Latin and Eastern Churches • The significant ecclesial renewal confirmed by the Second Vatican Council: the Church as sacrament, mystery, communion, and mission; the People of God; the universal call to holiness; privileges and responsibilities of the baptized community of disciples in mission; and the role of the ordained and lay faithful • Mariology and the communion of saints • The role of the Holy Spirit in the Church and in the world as unifier • Catholic doctrine and belief as presented in Catholic Tradition, the documents of Vatican II, the *Catechism of the Catholic Church*, and other relevant church documents • The use of theological sources to ground, interpret, and guide the activity that constitutes the pastoral dimension of the life of the Church	• To explain the Church's heritage and history and communicate the teaching of the Magisterium faithfully • To explain these foundational images of the Church described by the Second Vatican Council, especially to adults • To explain the place of Mary and the saints in the life of the Church and in an authentic Catholic Christian spirituality • To reflect upon and explain the presence and role of the Holy Spirit in the Church and world • To teach, evangelize, preach, and catechize about the foundations of the Catholic faith and doctrine, as well as convey the basic teachings of the Church faithfully and appropriately • To interpret the meaning and value of pastoral life in light of the ecclesiology of Vatican II; to enable people to identify and share these meanings more consciously in their lives

Appreciation/Knowledge of	Demonstrated Ability/Skill
10. Worship, Liturgy, and Sacrament	
• The history and essential principles of the Church's liturgical and sacramental life	• To explain the history and meaning of the liturgy and sacramental rites of the Church
• Liturgical principles, documents, and revised rites of the Church	• To use liturgical principles and documents in designing and leading learning sessions for adults as an immediate preparation for the Sacrament of Baptism, Eucharist, Reconciliation, Confirmation, Marriage, Eucharistic benediction, and Christian burial; to preside during the liturgy of the word in the absence of a priest; to help plan specific liturgical rites
• The variety of forms and styles of prayer and the difference between liturgical and private devotional prayer	
• The liturgical rites in which deacons participate; the meaning, structure, and implementation of the RCIA/RCIC	• To incorporate appropriate prayer experiences for different groups
• The theology of Holy Orders	• To provide authentic and credible witness in diaconal liturgical functions; to be familiar with the Church as envisioned in the RCIA and with *Study Text VI*
	• To articulate a theology of diaconate, in the context of the other orders, Tradition, history, the restoration at the Second Vatican Council, and the Rite of Ordination of Deacons

APPRECIATION/KNOWLEDGE OF	DEMONSTRATED ABILITY/SKILL

11. Moral Theology

- Scriptural, theological, philosophical, and psychological foundations and principles for Catholic moral teaching, conscience formation, and decision-making; Christian ethics
- The complex nature of moral and social issues
- Key concepts of Catholic morality found in the *Catechism of the Catholic Church*, Catholic social teaching, and contemporary theological reflection, especially John Paul II's encyclical letters *The Splendor of Truth* and *The Gospel of Life*, and the pastoral letters of the bishops of the United States

- To explain and teach a Catholic understanding of conscience and moral formation to individuals and groups to assist in the development of Christian consciences informed by God's word, magisterial teaching, and reason
- To apply Catholic moral principles to discussion of moral and social issues of our times, including abortion, euthanasia, capital punishment, abuse, war, sexuality, and economic justice
- To enable people to make moral decisions as Catholics in fidelity to Catholic moral teaching and principles; to develop a Catholic moral attitude and conscience

12. Canon Law

- *Book I: General Norms*: Canons 1 (Latin Rite only), 11 (subjects), 85 (dispensations), 96 (Apersonality@ in Church)
- *Book II: People of God*: Canons 204/205 (effects of Baptism), 206 (catechumens), 212 (triple munera), 215/216 (associations), 220/221 (privacy/defend rights), 233 (fostering vocations), 330/331 (Roman pontiff), 369 (diocese), 383 (role of bishop), 573/574 (religious life)
- Incardination/excardination; rights of clerics
- *Book III: Teaching Function*: Canons 747-750 (truth and teaching), 755 (ecumenism), 766 (preaching), 774 (parental role), 781 (mission mandate), 788 (catechumens), 793-796 (Catholic education)

- To understand that Baptism is a juridical act that incorporates one into the Church of Christ; to understand that ecclesiastical law obligates those who are baptized into the Roman Catholic Church; to demonstrate practical knowledge of who is affected by church law
- To demonstrate knowledge of the effects of Baptism of Christian faithful with emphasis on the role of the laity; to demonstrate knowledge of the basic hierarchical structures of the Church, the role of religious and all vocations, and the rights and duties of Christian faithful as expressed in the various roles and structures of the Church
- To demonstrate an understanding of what constitutes the

APPRECIATION/KNOWLEDGE OF

DEMONSTRATED ABILITY/SKILL

- *Book IV: Office of Sanctifying*: Canons 840 (nature of the sacraments), 842 (primacy of Baptism), 849 (Baptism: theology, form), 879/880 (Confirmation: theology, form), 897/899 (Eucharist: theology, form), 959/960 (Penance: theology, form), 998 (Anointing: theology, form), 1008/1009 (Orders: theology, formation, special attention to canons on permanent deacons), 1055/1061 (Matrimony: theology, essential properties and form for validity), 1186 (veneration of saints)
- *Book IV* (continued): Canons 851/852 (Baptism: preparation), 861 (Baptism: ministers), 868 (Infant Baptism), 873/874 (Baptism: sponsor), 877 (record of Baptism), 891 (Confirmation: age), 893 (Confirmation: sponsor), 895 (record of Confirmation), 919 (Eucharist: preparation), 961 (Penance: general absolution), 1108/1122 (Matrimony: valid form), 1124/1129 (Matrimony: mixed religious and disparity of cult), 1156/1160 (Matrimony: simple convalidation), 1171 (sacramentals), 1176-1177 (funeral rites), 1180/1184 (burial and records), 1246/1248 (Sunday, holyday observance)
- *Book IV* (continued): Canons 916 (Eucharist: state of grace), 917 (Eucharist: frequency), 983 (Penance: seal of), 987/988 (Penance: disposition), 1063 (Matrimony: marriage care), 1249/1250 (days of penance)

deposit of faith as handed down through Scripture and Tradition; to understand that the baptized are to proclaim the Gospel to all peoples according to each one's proper role in the Church, and in a spirit of ecumenism; to demonstrate practical knowledge of evangelization and the mandate of the Christian faithful to safeguard the ministry of the word; to understand the importance of Catholic education and its relationship to the parental role of furthering the mission of Christ
- To demonstrate functional knowledge of the sanctifying character and form of the seven ritual sacraments, the liturgy, and sacramentals; to understand the basic theology and essential form of the sacraments of the Church; to explain the use of sacramentals and the veneration of the saints
- To identify and understand the norms of the universal Church on the Sacrament of Matrimony so that an adequate and thorough preparation can be achieved for Christian couples in their celebration of a valid and licit marriage.
- To apply the norms of the universal Church in the design and implementation of sacramental catechesis and liturgical celebration; to understand canonical requirements for sacramental ministers, liturgical form, and proper reception of the sacraments; to understand the

APPRECIATION/KNOWLEDGE OF	DEMONSTRATED ABILITY/SKILL
• *Book V: Temporal Goods:* Canons 1262 (support of church), 1265 (fund raising), 1280/1283/1287 (administration) • *Book VI: Sanctions:* Canons 1323 (exemptions from penalty), 1324 (penalty lessened), 1398 (abortion) • *Book VII: Resource:* how to advise an individual of his or her rights within the Church and canonical processes available • How to revere and respect the individual and the community of Christian disciples	canonical guidelines for the use of sacramental and proper observance of Sunday and holy days • To apply the principles of rights, obligations, and interior disposition in catechizing and in ritual celebrations; to give appropriate instruction regarding rights and obligations and necessary dispensations for sacramental observances • To understand the responsibilities of good stewardship in supporting the works of the Church in respect to gifts, church property, and ecclesiastical goods; to demonstrate knowledge of criteria for responsible stewardship • To be cognizant of penalties attached to serious transgressions in the Church, and the pastoral applications of penalties; to demonstrate awareness of the conditions and circumstances affecting the application of penalties, especially a procured abortion • To be familiar with due process and tribunal ministry • To be familiar with the canonical bill of rights for all the baptized

APPRECIATION/KNOWLEDGE OF	DEMONSTRATED ABILITY/SKILL

13. New Evangelization, Catechesis, and Small Christian Communities

- The theological and scriptural foundations of Catholic evangelization and catechesis

- The aims, processes, and principles of evangelization; familiarity with U.S. bishops' strategies for evangelization in the United States in *Go and Make Disciples*

- Effective methods of evangelization and mission in outreach through relationship-building and witness

- Effective teaching as a catechist, especially among adults

- The nature and purpose of small Christian communities in the contemporary Church

- Relevant catechetical documents as well as diocesan sacramental standards and policies

- Effective catechetical methods for adult and youth religious formation

- To infuse evangelization and catechesis into all diaconal ministries
- To implement effective strategies for evangelization; to facilitate and motivate a Catholic witness in the world
- To preach the Gospel when convenient and inconvenient, especially in the marketplace and at home; to bear witness to the Gospel with one's whole life
- To articulate the basic tenets of the faith using appropriate catechetical pedagogy and methodologies that address the age, psychology, and needs of those being catechized
- To organize and support the organization, leadership, and spiritual development of small Christian communities
- To demonstrate familiarity with catechetical documents; universal, national, and diocesan policies; pedagogy; and methods to evaluate catechetical processes, programs, and personnel in light of these documents and policies
- To implement methods in preaching, teaching, and directing adult/youth learners; to relate Scripture and Creed, especially in preaching

Appreciation/Knowledge of	Demonstrated Ability/Skill
14. Catholic Identity, Ecumenism, and Interreligious Dialogue	
• The effort to recover the unity of all Christians as the gift of Christ and work of the Holy Spirit; the Church's mission *ad gentes*	• To develop relationships of understanding and respect with individuals of other Christian and non-Christian faiths while retaining his own Roman Catholic identity
• The common spiritual values shared by all believers and non-believers	• To articulate his own Catholic faith while identifying with other denominations and other religious traditions
• Similarities and differences among the Catholic tradition and other Christian traditions	• To provide learning opportunities to develop ecumenical knowledge, understanding, and openness, especially on the parochial level
• Jewish faith and tradition	• To articulate and appreciate our Catholic roots within Judaism
• Other non-Christian religious traditions and the gifts they bring to humankind	• To foster an appreciation for other religious traditions; to provide and participate in common dialogue, especially for collective social action
• Canon Law and other principles, guidelines, and magisterial teaching for Christian and interfaith dialogue, common action, prayer, and marriage	• To provide an authentic and effective ministry and presence in Christian and interfaith activities; to give leadership to opportunities for prayer and common action in response to human needs

APPRECIATION/KNOWLEDGE OF	DEMONSTRATED ABILITY/SKILL

Pastoral Dimension
15. Pastoral Theology

- How to connect the academic disciplines of theology with pastoral care

- The role/function of religion in people's lives

- Use of theological sources to ground, interpret, and guide the pastoral life of the Church

- Complex theological issues stemming from life experiences

- The role of theological reflection in pastoral ministry

- The theory and practice of social analysis in theological reflection

- To use theology as a help to analyze pastoral situations for an understanding of God's presence and will as articulated in Scripture, Tradition, and the magisterial teaching of the Church
- To demonstrate empathy in ministry, applying religious psychology and sociology
- To locate, select, and use appropriate sources for specific pastoral situations
- To reflect in an interdisciplinary way, using psychology, sociology, and cultural and theological disciplines in understanding issues confronting societies
- To facilitate a critical reflection on complex human and church pastoral issues doing theological reflection from within concrete experiences
- To use available resources to conduct social analysis, including the integration of the various levels of diocesan/parish diversity

APPRECIATION/KNOWLEDGE OF	DEMONSTRATED ABILITY/SKILL

16. Communication

- The importance and use of listening skills

- Self-expression skills

- Conflict management and confrontation

- How to direct effective meetings

- Group process and collaborative skills

- Public speaking skills, including organization of thoughts

- Sacraments and prayer in pastoral ministry and as primarily relational

- The needs of migrant and immigrant people; the role of hospitality, welcome, and service

- Competencies and limitations

- New technologies

- To employ good verbal and non-verbal communication skills; to be an empathetic, active listener, providing feedback and withholding and making judgments appropriately
- To express himself succinctly in a well-ordered and logical way, conveying his feelings and views yet remaining open to differing views with tolerance
- To discern the issues involved in conflict and promote appropriate resolution; to provide behavior-focused feedback
- To motivate and lead groups to set agendas collaboratively, manage time, set goals, and make decisions through consensus; to empower others with leadership skills
- To build groups of solidarity, cooperation, and trust through partnership and teamwork
- To speak in a clear, well-ordered, logical way; to use a variety of techniques and methods to support oral presentations
- To provide directly or by referral the resources of the Church and its tradition to the occasions of pastoral care
- To demonstrate multicultural sensitivity; to provide appropriate spiritual and physical response
- To not act beyond his level of training in each pastoral care situation; to know when, how, and to whom appropriate referrals should be made
- To be familiar with the Internet, especially distance learning, through online seminars and interactive conferencing

APPRECIATION/KNOWLEDGE OF	DEMONSTRATED ABILITY/SKILL

17. Human Development and Conversion

- The stages of human development: physiological, psychological, cultural, spiritual, intellectual, emotional, sexual, moral, and social

- Various theories of faith development, especially in youth and adult formation

- How major cultural and family trends and values affect human development

- Dynamics of conversion

- Role of personal prayer

- The needs of persons with physical or developmental disabilities

- Cultural and family mythologies and practices of those to whom he ministers

- To apply appropriate human development principles in preaching, programming, and counsel
- To utilize appropriate models of faith formation in preaching, programming, and counsel
- To assess and utilize the family, social, cultural, and global trends and concerns in developing appropriate pastoral ministries and in preaching
- To identify, articulate, and foster personal and communal conversion experiences
- To demonstrate regular commitment to a pattern of personal prayer and to support others' growth in prayer
- To appreciate, understand, and include groups and/or individuals with physical or developmental disabilities in a variety of pastoral programming and activities, especially in Eucharistic liturgies and religious formation; to be familiar with the U.S. bishops' pastoral letter *Welcome and Justice for Persons with Disabilities*

- *18. Pastoral Care, Assessment, and Intervention*
- The need for prudence in dealing with others, especially their personal lives

- Assessment and intervention skills

- Local resources for use in assessment, intervention, and referral

- To be empathetic, genuine, and respectful; to maintain confidentiality and objectivity; to apply basic counseling skills
- To discern if and when referral is necessary
- To identify competent resources in the parish, diocese, and societal community; to maintain an information, referral, and skill training network

APPRECIATION/KNOWLEDGE OF	DEMONSTRATED ABILITY/SKILL

19. Multicultural Sensitivities, Justice, Service, and the Option for the Poor

- Principles, processes, and models for the development of a justice consciousness; how to facilitate service outreach programs with emphasis on the preferential option for the poor

- How to develop diaconal ministries in the context of a multicultural church and society

- Traditions and faith expressions of different cultural groups; the role of culture in formation

- Cultural communication patterns and their impact in setting ministerial goals and programming

- To integrate justice and peace into his diaconal life, family, preaching, teaching, and staff organizational meetings; to attend to issues of homelessness, hunger, and AIDS; to model the interconnectedness of all people and, especially, to the earth (global ecology); to model a simple lifestyle; to stimulate reflective decision making and action for those in need; to discern appropriate societal response
- To demonstrate personal awareness and response to the needs of particular cultural/racial/ethnic communities
- To incorporate cultural expression of faith into diaconal preaching, service, and prayer experiences
- To use cultural communication patterns when appropriate; to create and support viable structures and strategies to foster diverse cultural and ethnic participation

20. Lay Leadership Formation and Development

- How to affirm and call forth the gifts of youth and adults and provide for their ongoing spiritual and leadership development
- The skills needed by volunteer ministerial leaders
- Resources to effectively call forth the gifts of the community for ministry

- To enable others to reflect upon and express their faith experiences
- To match gifts with ministry needs
- To utilize all types of media resource to recruit and facilitate ministerial leaders

APPRECIATION/KNOWLEDGE OF	DEMONSTRATED ABILITY/SKILL

21. Community Formation
- Principal elements for community building, activities, and process
- The richness of the community: images of the Church as People of God, mystery, sacrament, communion, mission, Mystical Body of Christ
- Basic communications and relational skills

- To create, in cooperation with the Holy Spirit in the midst of the world and the Church, an environment of hospitality and welcome for all gatherings within church and neighborhood
- To implement a community dimension into all structures for planning, programming, and evaluation
- To demonstrate patience and sensitivity in communicating with and relating to staff, families, and organizations

22. Leadership Processes and System Strategies
- How to work collaboratively with individuals and groups within and outside a diaconal assignment

- Necessary managerial principles and skills: e.g., pastoral planning, time management, financial management

- Principles for supervision and performance appraisal

- The dynamics of the role of leader

- Computer and Internet resources

- How to use media and technology in developing and implementing programs

- To recruit, train, support, supervise, and assess
- To apply appropriate managerial principles and administrative skills to design, implement, and coordinate programs; to employ needs assessment and analysis; to formulate mission statements, goals/objectives, strategies, and evaluation methods; to prepare and monitor budgets; to organize tasks by priority and organize and manage his time in accord with ministry requirements; to delegate responsibilities, including authority to act; to recognize stress and select methods to respond
- To develop and implement appropriate job descriptions; to set achievable performance goals; to supervise appraisals
- To engage in advocacy, mediation, referrals, and facilitation
- To demonstrate knowledge and skills in computer/internet applications, including online seminars
- To use media and technology for effective ministerial implementation

Appreciation/Knowledge of	Demonstrated Ability/Skill
23. Ethical Standards	
• Liabilities pertinent to ministry: confidentiality, insurance issues, harassment, etc.	• To engage in employment agreements through familiarity with canonical and civil law pertaining to rights of individuals and employees relating to hiring, evaluation, dismissal, and abuse issues; to establish positive support systems and referral networking; to conduct information programs so that these basic rights and responsibilities are affirmed and cherished
• Liabilities relating to personal conduct in ministry	• To establish prudent and appropriate boundaries for interpersonal conduct, especially with women and youth

APPRECIATION/KNOWLEDGE OF

Diaconal Vocation and Ministry
24. Ministerial Identity & Vocation

- The role of the deacon in the life and mission of the diocesan and parochial Church and the esteemed tradition of deacons in the Church
- The background of the restoration and the implementation of the diaconate in the context of the Second Vatican Council, the writings of Paul VI, the teachings of John Paul II, the *Basic Norms and Directory for the Ministry and Life of Permanent Deacons* (published by the Congregations for Catholic Education and for the Clergy) and the *National Directory* of the U.S. bishops
- His call to the diaconate and a commitment to living the Gospel in all aspects of life
- The dynamics of the role of leadership in today's Church as a member of the clergy and participant in the hierarchy
- The deacon's mission in the marketplace in society

DEMONSTRATED ABILITY/SKILL

- To effectively proclaim the Gospel; to be recognized at the altar as the sacrament of Jesus, the Deacon-Servant, in the midst of the community, and as herald of the word, sanctifier in liturgy, and advocate for the poor as minister of charity and justice
- To instruct and catechize others about the diaconate and its mission as "the Church's service sacramentalized"
- To witness to Christ in living, giving, and empowering ways; to articulate his call to diaconate as vocation; to identify, call forth, affirm, and support the gifts and talents of others
- To help others to grow in their knowledge of the faith and personal holiness; to animate, facilitate, and motivate the whole Church ministry of charity and justice; to collaborate with others in leadership in diocesan and parochial ministries; to mediate or manage conflict; to make decisions and monitor outcomes; to witness to The Gospel of Life by an exemplary life and service
- To witness to the Gospel in his place of employment; to understand the implication of political decisions in view of the Gospel and the social justice teaching of the Church; to sensitize God's people with an informed social consciousness; to evangelize non-Christians and Christians

APPRECIATION/KNOWLEDGE OF	DEMONSTRATED ABILITY/SKILL

25. Ministry of the Word

- Relationship of Scripture, doctrine, and revelation

- How to proclaim the moral and social teachings of the Church

- How to catechize the faithful on the basic truths of the Church

- How to evangelize non-Catholic neighbors and non-Christians

- To prepare a proper exegesis and contemporary application of the biblical text(s); apply the biblical text(s) with the Tradition and teaching of the Church to issues confronting the community today

- To preach on matters of faith and morals, Christ's initiation, and our response, expressing himself clearly and easily in a manner appropriate to the occasion; to be sensitive to the varied cultural, ethnic, racial, and gender dynamics of the text and the message

- To utilize the skills for an effective homiletic or catechetical presentation through frequent social gospel preaching; to inform the community of their obligation to respond to the needs of the poor and to serve as Jesus did; to give personal witness; to speak the Gospel in his place of employment and in the marketplace with boldness, linking the sanctuary to the neighborhood, as well as the needs of the neighborhood to the sanctuary; to organize business leaders and neighbors around the Gospel, even on an ecumenical basis

- To evangelize, drawing from the U.S. bishops' statement *Go and Make Disciples*, as well as from the writings of Pope Paul VI and Pope John Paul II on evangelization

APPRECIATION/KNOWLEDGE OF	DEMONSTRATED ABILITY/SKILL
26. Ministry of Liturgy • How to lead liturgical and sacramental celebrations • How to assist at Eucharistic celebrations • Liturgical directives and rites • How to prepare and plan for sacramental celebrations	• To lead and/or provide for Baptisms, communion services, burial services, weddings, non-sacramental reconciliation rites, devotions, and Sunday celebrations in the absence of a priest as a liturgical presider • To exercise the ministry of deacon in Eucharistic celebrations; to identify the table of Eucharist with the table of the poor, bringing their needs to the common prayers of intercession • To exercise his role in conformity with the Church's liturgical directives • To collaborate with the pastor, other priests and deacons, worship committees, and liturgical ministers in planning and implementing the liturgy; to provide effective baptismal and marriage preparations in accordance with canonical norms and directives of the diocesan Church; to guide liturgical planning; to coordinate liturgical ministers or enable others to exercise that role

APPRECIATION/KNOWLEDGE OF	DEMONSTRATED ABILITY/SKILL
27. Ministry of Charity and Justice • The direct care of those in need • Advocacy for those in need • Education of the community • How to witness to charity and justice	• To serve in charitable care the needs of the poor, homeless, elderly, imprisoned, ill (including people with AIDS), and the marginalized of any kind • To create an environment of hospitality toward all people, especially the stranger and the marginalized; to join in coalition with other religious and secular groups for common political and community-based action; to integrate justice themes into his life and ministry • To provide educational programs that will assist the parish in understanding social justice as constitutive of the Gospel; to promote just parish structures; to situate study, reflection, and decision-making in the context of a responsibility to his world, especially to those in need; to participate in local debates and community action on behalf of those who are homeless, unemployed, suffering from AIDS, abused, etc. • To model and encourage simple living and environmental values; to preach justice by example and word; to demonstrate familiarity with the needs of the people in the community; to participate in charitable organizations; to be an advocate and servant of the poor; to promote justice and human development in local socio-economic situations; to minister to migrant and immigrant communities

SECONDARY DOCUMENT

VISIT OF CONSULTATION TEAMS TO DIOCESAN PERMANENT DIACONATE FORMATION PROGRAMS

Sixth Revision
Bishops' Committee on the Diaconate
December 2004

PREFACE

This document contains two parts that are closely related yet separate in their application. Included are:

1. The text of the December 2004 Sixth Revision of the Bishops' Committee on the Diaconate (BCD) *Policy Statement: Visit of Consultation Teams to Diocesan Diaconate Programs*.
2. A *Self-Study Instrument*

The Sixth Revision of this BCD *Policy Statement* is based on the 2004 *National Directory for the Formation, Ministry, and Life of Permanent Deacons in the United States*.

The *Policy Statement* is provided as a guide for a diocesan bishop who wishes formally to request a visit of a BCD Consultation Team. Such a visit is an opportunity for dialogue, discussion, and consultation which is summarized in a Consultation Team report to the requesting bishop. The report is confidential in nature. It becomes the property of the requesting bishop to be distributed and used at his discretion. It is offered as a service to a bishop and those to whom he has given the responsibility for the formation of deacons and the post-ordination life and ministry of deacons.

The *Self-Study Instrument* is a guide for a diocese to reflect on the experience of the diaconate and a self-critique of the degree of implementation of the provisions of the United States Conference of Catholic Bishops' 2004 *National Directory for the Formation, Ministry, and Life of Permanent Deacons in the United States*. Such a self-study could be implemented at times when the need becomes evident or as part of the preparation for a visit by a BCD Consultation Team. In that case, the self-study should be accomplished in advance of requesting such a visit. The results should be part of the materials provided to the Consultation Team as they prepare for their visit. The provisions of Appendix I (*Specific Normative Elements in Diaconal Formation*) to the *National Directory* apply.

The members of the Bishops' Committee on the Diaconate hope that these documents will help to strengthen diocesan programs of formation and post-ordination continuing education and spiritual formation of deacons.

Part I

POLICY STATEMENT

VISIT OF CONSULTATION TEAMS
TO DIOCESAN DIACONATE PROGRAMS
Sixth Revision
December 2004

I. Introduction

A. The diaconate is an integral part of the entire Christian Community. By means of the document *National Directory for the Formation, Ministry, and Life of Permanent Deacons in the United States* (*ND*), the bishops of the United States wish to ensure on the part of all involved a more effective preparation for and post-ordination support of diaconal ministry.

> As implemented in accord with local or regional resources, this *Directory* will provide a sure directive for promoting harmony and unity in diaconal formation and ministry throughout the United States and its territorial sees. In so doing, this *Directory* will ensure certain uniformity in the identity, selection, and formation of deacons, as well as provide for more clearly defined pastoral objectives in diaconal ministries. (ND, no. 292)

B. The diocesan program for diaconal formation and post-ordination support of deacons are under the immediate supervision of the diocesan bishop, his diocesan director of the diaconate, and other personnel to whom the bishop has entrusted areas of responsibility. To assist diocesan supervisory personnel in the on-going process of improving diaconal formation and making more effective the post-ordination support of deacons, the Bishops' Committee on the Diaconate (BCD) provides this policy statement and appends a suggested *Self-Study Instrument*.

C. One purpose of a visit of a consultation team and a self-study is to assist diocesan personnel to interpret and implement the *National*

Directory. A consultation team can also serve as a two-way channel of information, from diocesan program personnel to the Bishops' Committee and from the Bishops' Committee to the diocese concerning how best to prepare, support, and sustain a deacon and, if married, his wife and family.

D.   Earlier revised editions of this policy statement focused on the utilization of a consultation team for improving a diocesan program of formation. This Sixth Revision enlarges the scope of the team to consult on post-ordination continuing education and spiritual formation of deacons and it adds a self-study instrument This instrument may be employed by diocesan personnel either for diocesan use or in preparation for a visit of a BCD Consultation Team.

E.   The BCD Consultation Team is not an accrediting agent. The members of the team function in a diaconal spirit as collaborators with the diocesan bishop, program director, staff, and members of the diaconal community. The common goal is to achieve the objectives of the *National Directory* in adapting them to respond to the needs of the diocese so the deacons will prove to be of assistance to all who share the burden and the privilege of representing the Servant Christ to the Servant Church. (ND, nos. 14-17)

F.   Dioceses are encouraged to use the self-study instrument as a guide for an internal evaluation or as part of a process to determine whether or not a visit of a BCD Consultation Team is warranted.

G.   Circumstances that could warrant a request for a consultation team include the following:
1.   When a deacon formation is to be introduced or substantially modified
2.   When major program changes are contemplated
3.   When activating a program which has been "on hold" for more than two years
4.   When a new bishop has been appointed to a diocese
5.   After every ten years of formation activity
6.   When implementing or modifying a post-ordination program of supervision and support of deacons, their wives and families (no. 14; 16)

II. Initiating a Request for a Consultation Team Visit

A.   The process begins with a written invitation by a diocesan bishop to the chairman, Bishops' Committee on the Diaconate, requesting that the BCD provide a Consultation Team to visit his diocese. A choice of three dates should accompany the request. Ordinarily, a minimum of six months should be allowed between the invitation and the beginning of the visit of the Consultation Team. In the event that a deacon formation program is established in a religious institute, the invitation for a team visit would come from the major superior.

B.   In his invitation, the requesting bishop should specify his reason(s) for requesting the consultation so that team members will have clear guidance concerning the reason for their visit. If possible, the visitation should be timed to take advantage of scheduled diaconate events. The character of the formation program and the development of the diaconate in the requesting diocese will provide a basis for the scope of the consultation, and local circumstances will be considered in determining the composition of the team.

III. BCD Response to a Consultation Request

A.   Upon receipt o f the requesting bishop's invitation in the Secretariat, the assembling of the Consultation Team is the responsibility of the Executive Director. When composition of the Team is completed, the names will be proposed to the requesting bishop for his approval.

B.   Members of the Consultation Team should possess competence in the areas of spiritual, pastoral, and academic formation, as well as an understanding of various types of program administration. The character of the diaconate of the requesting diocese should be taken into account: regional, ethnic, social identity, administrative, or any other factors which distinguish a program's goal or process.

C.   The chair of the Consultation Team will be a bishop who is a present or past member of the Bishops' Committee on the Diaconate. Team members will include two directors of active diocesan deacon programs, one of whom is a deacon, and a deacon couple who are active in pastoral ministry. Ideally, all team members will be from dioceses where there is an active diaconate program If the situation requires it and the requesting diocese has the financial means of funding, additional personnel will complement the members of the Consultation Team.

D.   Every effort will be made to include one person who has served previously on a consultation team. Because of previous experience, the chair could utilize this person as a Special Facilitator. This Facilitator could help the diocesan director prepare for the consultation through conference calls, FAX, e-mail, or letter, especially in standardizing or streamlining the process of preparing the documentation needed by the team and in the scheduling of persons or groups who will participate in the consultation.

    a.   Once the composition of the team has been accepted by the requesting diocesan bishop, communication relation to the Team visit and consultation will be between the Team chair and the requesting bishop and his diocesan director of the diaconate. The Team chair will consult with his Team members concerning arrival times at the consultation site and estimated times of completion of the Team visit. These times will be coordinated with the requesting bishop and his diocesan director of the diaconate.

IV. Diocesan Preparations for a Consultation

A.   At least one month in advance of the visitation, the diocese will prepare a Background Questionnaire, a copy of which is appended to this *Policy Statement* as Appendix A.

B.   In addition, the following materials must be provided to each Consultation Team member so they might initiate internal team planning in advance of their visit:

1.   A statement describing how the deacon formation program and post-ordination programs of continuing education and spiritual formation conform to the provisions of the 2004 *National Directory*.
2.   The results of a self-study, based on the response to the questions outlined in a *Self-Study Instrument*, a copy of which follows this *Policy Statement*.
3.   Published materials that describe the deacon formation program, including the original design for formation, diaconal life, and ministry previously approved by the BCD; any revisions of the original design, which could include course descriptions, program bulletins, the results of previous self-studies, evaluations, and recommendations that may have emanated from them; goals and plans for future programming; and copies of minutes from recent board meetings.

C.   The requesting diocesan bishop and the Team chair will collaborate, as necessary, in planning for the consultation progresses.

D.   The diaconate staff of the requesting diocese will arrange local transportation, housing, and meals for the Consultation Team members throughout their visit.

V. Individuals and Groups to be Consulted

A.   In planning the schedule for the Consultation Team visit, the diaconate staff of the requesting diocese will identify those individuals or groups to be interviewed by Team members during their visit. The following individuals/groups are suggested:

1.   The diocesan bishop, other bishops, Vicar General, Chancellor, religious superiors
2.   Deacons and wives, either together or separately
3.   Deacon candidates and wives, either together or separately
4.   Children of permanent deacons and candidates, when available and appropriate
5.   Formation program faculty, including staff of a wives' program if integral to the program
6.   Diaconate and formation board members;
7.   Other diocesan personnel deemed appropriate by diocesan planners
8.   Representatives of deacon structure (council, assembly, etc.)
9.   A cross-section of priests, men and women religious, and laity who collaborate with deacons in ministry
10.   Pastors and others who supervise deacons in ministry

B.   In conferring with the above persons, Team members will take into consideration the various relationships they have to the deacon formation program and to diaconal ministry in the diocese.

C.   In assigning Team members for interviews, the Team chair will give consideration to the effectiveness of peer interviews—bishop to bishop, diaconate director to diaconate director, wife of deacon to wives of deacons, priest to priest, deacon to deacon.

VI. Conducting the Consultation

A. Purpose

1. To provide the diocesan bishop with an assessment of the diocesan program of formation and the post-ordination life and ministry of deacons, based on principles contained in the 2004 *National Directory*, as adapted and implemented to respond to the needs of his diocese
2. To offer constructive suggestions or recommendations to help strengthen the programs or make them more effective
3. To help interpret current trends in diaconal ministries
    4. To serve as a channel of communication for the Bishops' Committee on the Diaconate

B. Methods

The consultation process will be guided by one basic question, How is the diocesan diaconate fulfilling its objectives in light of the *National Directory*, taking into consideration the suggestions, recommendations, or conditions made by the Bishops' Committee on the Diaconate at the time of their approval of the diocese's diaconal program?

The diocesan staff and Consultation Team members will focus their efforts on the following questions:

1. What are the goals of the formation program?
2. What is the content of the formation program in each of the areas outlined in the USCCB *National Directory*? (see Part II *Self-Study*)
3. How is the *National Directory* being implemented and adapted in each of the above areas?
4. What educational and formational processes described in the *National Directory* are utilized or have been adapted for use in the diocesan diaconate program?
5. How have these processes been adapted to meet the geographic, cultural, ethnic, educational, and ministerial needs and resources of the diocese?
6. How effective are the processes used by the diaconal formation program in achieving its goals?

C. Duration of Consultation Visit

Ordinarily, a period of at least three full days should be spent evaluating a diaconate program by the Consultation Team. A fourth day is optional and may be scheduled, if deemed necessary, by the Team. During the visit, the members of the Team should try to participate, as fully as possible, in the diaconal community life. In the case when a "weekend format" is used for the consultation, the visit would be scheduled on a regular formation weekend. In the case of a weekly "night school" format, a "class night" ideally would be included in the visitation.

In addition to the three-day Team visit, it could be helpful if one member, perhaps the Special Facilitator (see no. III D) could be present for a period of time, in advance of the others, to assist the diocesan staff in final preparations for the consultation.

Since the purpose of the consultation is for peer support and assistance, it is crucial that an atmosphere of total cooperation and mutual trust be fostered between members of the Consultation Team and the diaconal community.

D. Suggested Consultation Schedule

Each evening of the visit, the chair will assemble the Team to assess the work of the day and identify what remains to be done. Every effort should be made by the host personnel to house the Team members in one facility to reduce travel time and facilitate the Team's efforts. At times during the visit, private dinners for the Team alone may provide a relaxing respite from the rigorous schedule of the consultation and offer an opportunity for a bonding of the Team members. In addition, team meals give members a chance in a relaxed atmosphere to discuss various aspects and plans and schedule adjustments in the visitation process. Meals may also be shared with one or more of the groups to be interviewed or with the requesting bishop and other diocesan personnel.

An outline for a sample schedule is appended to this *Policy Statement* as Appendix B.

VII. Providing Feedback, Preliminary Reports, and the Final Consultation Report to the Requesting Bishop

A.   When giving feedback, preparing preliminary reports, or writing the final consultation Team report, the chair and Team members will distinguish between their objective observations of a diocesan program's compliance with the provisions of the *National Directory* and their personal observations. The Team's objective observations will provide the basis of the report on each area of the diaconal program, their commendations and recommendations, and the basis for the Team's final report of the consultation.

B.   During the consultation, Team members may make suggestions based on their own experience. Since the focus of the Consultation Team is an evaluation of a diocesan program's adherence to the provisions of the *National Directory*, however, any recommendations made to the diocesan staff will focus on helping the diaconate staff either to comply with or adapt the provisions of the *National Directory* to their specific needs.

C.   The preliminary oral report and the final written report of the Consultation Team provide a constructive assessment of the degree to which local implementation and adaptation of the *National Directory* have been made. Recommendations are offered to help strengthen deacon formation, post-ordination diaconal life, and ministry in the diocese. Subsequently, any changes made in a local program in order to implement the Team's recommendations will be determined by the diocesan bishop and carried out by the staff.

D.   Prior to the departure of the Consultation Team, a preliminary oral report will be made to the requesting diocesan bishop and/or his director of the diaconate and others the bishop may elect to invite. The manner and details of this presentation will be the responsibility of the Team chair. The oral report includes impressions and tentative conclusions of the Team members. This is the time to clarify any ambiguities, either on the part of the Team or of the requesting bishop and his staff.

E.   The final written report

1.   The requesting diocesan bishop should receive a written report within one month following the conclusion of the consultation.

2.   Each Team member will prepare a report on those areas of the program assigned to him or her. Duplications or possible contradictions will be minimized through consultation among Team members. Each Team member should send a typed copy of his/her report of assigned areas of responsibility directly to the Team chair within one week of the conclusion of the consultation.

3.   The Team chair will assemble an integrated report, objective and based on fact, and a brief introduction to the report.

4.   Each section of the report should consist of three parts:

-   A general description
-   Commendations (highlighting program strengths)
-   Recommendations (action to bring formation and post-ordination diaconal life and ministry into conformity with the provisions of the 2004 *National Directory*)

5.   The Team Report is mailed to the Secretariat where it is reproduced and distributed to the Committee members for their comments, and approval/disapproval When approved, the report will be sent to the Diocesan Bishop under a cover letter from the chairman, BCD. The report then becomes the property of the requesting diocesan bishop, to be utilized as he sees fit.

VIII. Reimbursement and Remuneration

A.   The requesting diocese is expected to cover the following costs of Team members:

- Transportation
- Accommodations
- Miscellaneous expenses (meals, airport transfers, etc.)
- Stipend of $50 per day for each team member

B.   Consultation Team members will submit supporting documents to a person designated by the requesting bishop within seven days following the Team's visit Reimbursement of Team members and payment of the stipend should be accomplished within thirty days following completion of the consultation visit. A suggested reimbursement form is appended to this *Policy Statement* as Appendix C.

C.   As a matter of justice, the wife of the deacon is considered an individual member of the Consultation Team. Her stipend will be independent of that of her deacon husband.

APPENDIX A

Background Questionnaire for Visit of Consultation Team

Bishops' Committee for the Diaconate

This completed questionnaire should accompany the initial request from a diocese when requesting a Consultation Team Visit to a local diaconate program. A similar cover sheet accompanies the self-study instrument, which is submitted prior to the visitation.

Date _____

(Arch)Diocese _____

Diocesan (Arch)Bishop _____

Address _____

_____

Telephone, FAX _____

E-mail _____

Address, Telephone, FAX, E-mail of the Office of the Permanent Diaconate, if different from above _____

_____

Preferred Dates Desired for visitation

(1) _____ (2) _____ (3) _____

Diaconate Director (s)

(Title/Name) _____

(Title/Name) _____

(Title/Name) _____

(Title/Name) _____

Local Diocesan Structure for Permanent Deacons, e.g. Board, Association, etc.

_____

Number of Permanent Deacons in Diocese _____

Current Formation Program   ❐ Yes   ❐ No

If yes, number of candidates in formation _____

Date Deacon Formation first began in diocese _____

Is copy of original approved program available?   ❐ Yes   ❐ No

Length of Program of Formation _____

Model of Program of Formation (weekly, monthly, urban, rural, cultural factors, etc)

Site of Formation Program (facility & location) _____

Diaconate Formation Staff and their Qualifications

Human Formation

Academic/Intellectual Formation

Spiritual Formation

Pastoral Formation/Field Education

Program for Wives

Please indicate what circumstances warrant a request for a consultation team visit at this time.

❐ Diaconal formation program is being introduced under 2004 *Directory*

❐ Diaconal formation program has been substantially modified under 2004 *Directory*

❐ Diaconal formation program changes are contemplated in the future

❐ Activating a formation program which has been "on hold" for more than two years

❐ A new bishop has been appointed to the diocese

❐ The formation program has been active for ten years

❐ The program of supervision and support of permanent deacons, their wives, and their families is being implemented or modified

The name, address and phone number of person responsible for paying the travel, room and board, and stipend (suggested $50.00 per day per member) for each member of the Consultation Team. See Appendix C for

Reimbursement Report.

Name _____

Address _____

Phone Number _____

E-Mail _____

APPENDIX B
Sample Schedule

At the discretion of the consulting team and the diocesan staff, the following sample schedule may be adjusted for a weekday or weekend consultation, or for an urban or rural program.

Day of Arrival

Arrival of team in time for a 5:00 p.m. meeting to discuss the visitation schedule and to review preliminaries on the *Self-Study*. The team will determine the division of work for the visit, emphasizing the use of the *National Directory* as the basis for the consultation.

Evening: Orientation meeting with the diocesan bishop and/or the diaconate director(s)

Purposes: To provide an overview of the diocese, a history of the diaconate in that diocese, and to determine to whom the final oral report is to be given.

First Day

A.M.:   Meeting with the formation faculty and diaconate program staff (e.g. coordinators of the theological, spiritual, and pastoral formation components, coordinator of wives' program, coordinator (s) for specific ethnic and cultural programs, etc.)

Purposes: To discuss the goals and objectives, developments, and concerns of the programs' leadership regarding diaconal formation, post-ordination support, and the ministry and life of permanent deacons.

P.M.:   Peer interviews between bishops, diaconate directors, priests, candidates, deacons, wives, and children, etc. (see VI, D)

Purposes: For team members and diocesan staff to discuss in depth their responsibilities, observations, and concerns.

Evening: The team will review the areas that have been investigated, plan the division of work for the following day, and identify areas for further exploration and evaluation.

Second Day

A.M.:   Visitation of formation and continuing education classes, ministry settings, and communities served by the diaconate. When possible, determine selection of classes and pastoral experiences to be observed, by consultation with diaconate administrative staff, but not necessarily restricted to these.

Purposes: 1. To establish first-hand contact with the processes/settings for learning diaconal ministry.
2. To determine the quality of teaching in the formation program. These visits, together with participation in the liturgy, validate the self-study and verbal accounts provided by the diocesan staff.

Meetings with other resource personnel. They could be invited to came to a central location such as a diocesan or parish center for these meetings.

Purposes: To complete the information-gathering phase of the team visit and to gain a thorough understanding of the diaconate in this setting.

Evening: The team will discuss the tentative commendations and recommendations that seem to be emerging from the investigation. The chair will stress the importance of completing the written report on time, and sending copies of it to the Secretariat for the Diaconate within two weeks of the visitation.

Third Day

A.M.:   Discussion and consensus among the members of the consulting team.

P.M.:   Preliminary oral report to the diocesan bishop, directors, and perhaps others, determined by the bishop. This report will consist of preliminary observations. It will be factual in nature and will not involve any final evaluative judgment, nor will it invite any kind of response other than to clarify factual and observable information.

Fourth Day (Optional)

This day may be utilized to complete additional segments of the visit, for team members to prepare their reports, or for the chair to give the preliminary oral report, as described above. Team departs.

APPENDIX C

Reimbursement Report
Consultation Team Visit

Bishops' Committee on the Diaconate

Upon completion of the Consultation Visit, each team member fills out this form to account for and request remuneration of expenses incurred as part of the consultation team visit. The member mails the request within seven days to the diocesan office of the diaconate at the site of the visit or to the person/office designated by the host diocese. A copy is also mailed to the USCCB Secretariat for the Diaconate. The diocese arranges for reimbursement within thirty (30) days.

Date _____

Team Member Name _____

Address _____

City, State, Zip _____

Telephone(s) _____

FAX _____ E-MAIL _____

Site (Diocese) of Visit _____

Dates of Visit _____

Expenses Incurred (attach receipts)

Airfare   _____

Auto (.304 per mile) or Rental   _____

Stipend ($50.00 per day)   _____

Miscellaneous Expenses

+Meals   _____

+Airport Transfers   _____

+Other Expenses (be specific)   _____

TOTAL EXPENSES   _____

-ADVANCES RECEIVED   _____

TOTAL REIMBURSEMENT   _____

Signed _____   Approved _____
(Consultation Team Member)   (Diocesan Personnel)

cc: USCCB Secretariat for the Diaconate

Part II

Self-Study Instrument

Visit of Consultation Teams to
Diocesan Diaconate Programs
Sixth Revision
December 2004

The *Self-Study Instrument* is designed to guide each diocese in a thorough assessment of its diaconate programming, using the 2004 *National Directory for the Formation, Ministry, and Life of Permanent Deacons in the United States.*

The *Self-Study Instrument* may be completed independently by a diocese as an internal assessment of compliance with the *National Directory*. It is always prepared as part of the visit of a BCD Consultation Team, which is described separately in the *Policy Statement.*

Within the context of this *National Directory*, Appendix I *Specific Normative Elements in Diaconal Formation* highlights elements to plan, implement, and evaluate a diaconal program. In this *Self-Study Instrument*, the number(s) in parentheses all refer to paragraph numbers in the *National Directory.*

When a bishop submits a proposal to the Bishops' Committee on the Diaconate for review, he should provide descriptive information on the normative elements for formation, ministry, and life of deacons as outlined in Appendix I of the *National Directory*, which is included with this self-study instrument.

Each section of the *Self-Study Instrument* then goes on to assesses the diocese's compliance with or adaptation of the norms established by the BCD, which are described in parallel sections of the *National Directory.*

In completing a *Self-Study Instrument*, questions may be answered individually or answers may be combined in narrative form to achieve greater continuity. Additional descriptive information may be added to what is elicited by the *Self-Study Instrument* in order to more accurately present the diaconate program of a diocese.

APPENDIX I

Specific Normative Elements in Diaconal Formation

I. Introduction

This section has been added to highlight the specific normative elements that ought to be part of the planning, implementation, and evaluation of a diaconal program. They need to be interpreted within the intent and context of this *Directory*.

II. Specific Normative Elements to Include in a Proposal for Review

When a bishop submits a proposal to the Bishops' Committee on the Diaconate for review, he should provide descriptive information on the following normative elements for the formation, ministry, and life of deacons:

- The diocesan pastoral plan clarifying the deacon's identity, role, and function in diocesan pastoral ministry
- The catechesis on the diaconate, covering content and process for its clergy, religious and lay staff, and the lay faithful of the diocese
- The organization and structures established within the diocese
- The academic/professional competencies, including the names and background of the administration, primary faculty, mentors, and other formation personnel selected to plan and implement the program, as well as the orientation program for the staff to the diaconate and diaconal formation
- The recruitment process, a collaborative activity of the departments for vocations, diaconal formation, and parochial pastors
- The recruitment processes to be employed in inviting applicants from communities reflecting the ethnic, racial, and cultural diversity of the diocese, including a copy of recruiting guidelines, materials, and application forms
- The screening procedures, particularly the psychological and personality testing that may be used—a list of the instruments, how they will be interpreted, and by whom

- The selection process, including the advisory structures that will make recommendations to the bishop, particularly the committee on admission and scrutinies, with its proposed composition and charter, if available
- The incorporation of the human, spiritual, intellectual, and pastoral dimensions of each path in diaconal formation; the engagement of participants in the pastoral ministries of the diocese and specific parishes
- The aspirant path in formation, specifying program length, formation contact hours, general content, the model of formation chosen, linkage with other diocesan formation programs (if any), assessment procedures, a list of those who will guide this path in formation and their professional competencies, and the aspirant's handbook (if available)
- The candidate path in formation, specifying program length, formation contact hours, course descriptions, and methodology in compliance with the directives specified in the *Basic Norms for the Formation of Permanent Deacons* and this *Directory*, a list of the faculty and their academic/professional competencies, the model(s) chosen for formation, assessment procedures, a list of prescribed textbooks, and the candidate's handbook (if available)
- A declaration from the bishop regarding the verification of courses of study obtained through distance learning or Internet seminars
- The program for spiritual formation in each path in formation; the name and competencies of the spiritual director
- The level and content of the involvement of wives and families in the formation program, including any requirement policy for wives' participation
- The deacon personnel director and his competencies; the structures envisioned for the post-ordination path in formation; the provisions for the pastoral care of deacons in their ministry and life after ordination; the program for the newly ordained; supervision and review of the decree of appointment; assessment procedures; continuing spiritual, intellectual, and pastoral formation, as well as personalized training; ongoing formation programming for wives and families; special care for deacons who are ill, widowed, and retired, and also for widows of deacons; inclusion of deacons within diocesan structures; a copy of the form used in preparing the written ministerial agreement

- A description of the application of particular law governing deacons, as approved by the United States Conference of Catholic Bishops and applied within the diocese
- A copy of the deacon personnel policy handbook, with policies and procedures governing post-ordination diaconal ministry and life (if available)
- Plans for a regularly scheduled assessment of the formation program
- Procedures employed for maintaining a list of deacons with their ministerial assignments; pastoral care of retired or widowed deacons, as well as those living outside of the diocese

(*National Directory for the Formation, Ministry, and Life of Permanent Deacons in the United States*, Appendix I)

Administration

The establishment or renewal of diaconal ministry within a diocesan Church needs to be conceived and established within an overall diocesan plan for ministry in which the diaconate is seen as an integral component in addressing pastoral needs. In this way, deacons, who are ordained for service to the diocesan Church, will have a richer and firmer sense of their identity and purpose, as will those who collaborate in ministry with them. (*National Directory for the Formation, Ministry, and Life of Permanent Deacons in the United States*, no. 257)

1. How does the diaconate contribute to the overall pastoral plan of the diocese? (no. 257) How does the formation program prepare candidates to meet this need?

2. What is the mission of the permanent diaconate in the diocese? (no. 41) Are diocesan diaconal leaders familiar with the *National Directory for the Formation, Ministry, and Life of Permanent Deacons in the United States*? (nos. 14-17)

3. What is the operative definition of "deacon" in this local church? How are deacons utilized? (nos. 27-30)

4. How does the diaconate reflect the cultural reality and diversity of the local church? (nos. 144-145)

5. Describe what geographical, ethnic, and cultural demographics affect the style and formation of diaconal formation and ministry in the diocese (nos. 161-164).

6. Describe the ongoing efforts at catechesis in the diocese regarding diaconal ministry (no. 43).

7. What is the relationship of the diocesan diaconate office to the bishop? (nos. 41-47) Describe the responsibilities of the members of the diocesan diaconate staff. (nos. 271-276) What is the relationship of the faculty to the diocesan staff? to the candidates? (nos. 277-279) What are the responsibilities of any board related to the program of formation or post-ordination diaconal life and ministry? (nos. 281-291)

8. Describe the diocesan commitment to provide adequately trained personnel to administer the diaconate program? (nos. 281-291)

For the Administration category, please check the rating which best describes your overall assessment.

❒ A. Programs, plans, and activities are adequate or better than adequate in this category.

❒ B. Additional development and/or revision is needed in the following components of this category.
Indicate number(s) _____

❒ C. This category will require significant restructuring and/ or redesign.

The Formation Program
for Aspirancy, Candidacy, and Post-Ordination, and the Dimensions—Human, Spiritual, Intellectual, and Pastoral (including Liturgical Components)—of the Formation Program

1. What are the goals and objectives of the program of formation for aspirancy, candidacy, and ongoing formation? Describe the program of formation for each of the areas listed. How does each area of the program implement the *National Directory?* Describe the strengths and weaknesses in each of these areas (nos. 104-133; 188-197; 214-219; 241-249).

2. How is each path and dimension integrated with the others? How does each path and dimension contribute to (a) the spiritual development of the candidate? (b) the formation of community? (c) the service dimension of diaconate? (d) the pastoral dimension of diaconate? Does each year of formation include a social justice component that is integrated with different academic subjects? (nos. 149-150) How is this integration achieved? (nos. 188-197; 214-219)

3. Describe how the model of the formation program and its content is adapted to the geographical, social, economic, and cultural circumstances of the diocesan church, as characterized by the availability of staff and resources (nos. 144-145; 161–164; 261-265).

4. How are educational approaches used, consistent with effective methods of adult education? What adaptations are made through creative uses of modem technology, teaching techniques, instructional materials, traveling teams, etc? (no. 73; 74)

5. How are the needs of the society and culture in which candidates will be serving identified? What preparation is given to respond to such specific needs? (nos. 161-164)

6. Describe how subjects listed for each area of formation meet the needs of the local church and cultures, and are integrated with the formation program (nos. 193-197).

7. Who constitutes the faculty for the program of formation? What are their qualifications? What arrangements exist for the faculty to meet regularly for planning and feedback regarding the candidates? (nos. 277-279)

8. Describe what opportunities are provided for candidates to form small communities in order to take part in theological reflection (no. 133).

9. Describe the field education and internship opportunities offered during the formation program (no. 132; 197; 219).

10. Describe what opportunities are provided for practicums and gaining competency in pastoral ministry skills, homiletics, liturgy, and as a public leader of prayer (no. 130).

11. If the formation program is accredited in some manner, describe how this is accomplished.

For the Formation Program during Aspirancy, Candidacy, and Post-Ordination: Human, Spiritual, Intellectual and Pastoral Dimensions ('including Liturgical Components) category, please check the rating which best describes your overall assessment.

❐ A. Programs, plans, and activities are adequate or better than adequate in this category.
❐ B. Additional development and/or revision is needed in the following components of this category.
Indicate number(s) _____
❐ C. This category will require significant restructuring and/ or redesign.

Vocation, Discernment, and Selection of Candidates

1. What written materials or opportunities for catechesis exist for potential applicants to receive accurate information about the diaconate? How are potential candidates identified? (nos. 159-160)

2. In the admissions process, how are the following criteria determined for each applicant? (nos. 165; 173; 66.16)
   • a maturing Christian faith
   • personal integrity
   • appropriate maturity
   • holiness
   • regular participation in the Church's sacramental life
   • evidence of previous and respected commitment to the Church's life and service
   • a stable marriage and family life

3. Describe other criteria (level of education, age, etc.) necessary for an applicant to be favorably considered for acceptance into the diaconate formation program? (nos. 174-175; 177)

4. What documents are all applicants required to provide as part of their application? (no. 178)
   • certificates of Baptism, Confirmation, and if appropriate, marriage
   • health evaluation
   • if appropriate, written statement of wife's consent
   • letters of recommendation
   • age requirement
   • impediments; background check

5. What other documentation, interviews, and psychological assessment are required of applicants, and where appropriate, of their wives? (no. 178a-1)

6. What ethnic, cultural, and geographic considerations are made in the diaconate selection process? (nos. 161-162; 164)

7. Describe how wives are involved in the application and screening processes (no. 170).

8. Describe the process of discernment (nos. 165-166; 168; 169-173; 179).

9. How is the discernment of readiness for the aspirancy path assessed? Is this recommendation forwarded to the bishop for his approval? (nos. 179-181)

For the Vocation, Discernment, and Selection of Candidates category, please check the rating which best describes your overall assessment.

☐ A. Programs, plans, and activities are adequate or better than adequate in this category.
☐ B. Additional development and/or revision is needed in the following components of this category.
    Indicate number(s) _____
☐ C. This category will require significant restructuring and/or redesign.

Assessment and Evaluation During Formation

1. Describe how the local Church discerns and ratifies the call to diaconal ministry (nos. 153-154; 227-231; 243; 266; 284).

2. Describe the assessment processes used during the aspirancy and candidacy paths of formation. Who participates in the evaluation process? How does the evaluation process need to be strengthened? (nos. 198-200; 205; 209; 220-230)

3. Describe the criteria for assessing readiness to nominate into the candidate path. (nos. 198-203); human (no. 189); spiritual (nos. 191-195); intellectual (no. 196); pastoral (no. 197).

4. How are candidates held accountable for their performance in their theological/intellectual formation? (nos. 115-125)

5. What criteria are used for assessing the pastoral skills(including liturgical skills) of a candidate as a consideration of his fitness for ordination? (nos. 126-133)

6. How does the formation program help the candidate with the goals for spiritual development? (nos. 110-117)

7. What are the criteria for readiness for institution to the ministries of lector and acolyte? (nos. 232-234)

8. What are the criteria for assessing the candidate's suitability for ordination? How are candidates called to Orders? (nos. 225-231)

9. What processes are used following ordination to evaluate the deacon's ministry? How often and by whom? Are such evaluations made part of the deacon's permanent personnel recall in the diaconate office? (nos. 245-249)

For the Assessment and Evaluation category please check the rating which best describes your overall assessment.

❒ A. Programs, plans, and activities are adequate or better than adequate in this category.

❒ B. Additional development and/or revision is needed in the following components of this category.
Indicate number(s) _____

❒ C. This category will require significant restructuring and/or redesign.

Family Life Perspective

1. In what ways is the overall health of each candidate's marriage and family assessed during the selection process and throughout formation? (nos. 136-143; 175; 185; 190; 192; 198; 200; 212; 217e)

2. How does the program of formation address the issues of marriage and family? What effort is made to evaluate the home environment and family relationships of the candidates? (no. 175; 190; 212)

3. How are the wives and families included in the program of formation? (nos. 192; 234; 236-237)

4. How are the candidates' wives and children helped to understand and adjust to the demands of diaconal ministry undertaken by their husbands and fathers? (no. 44; 47)

5. What support exists to meet the needs of wives and children before and after ordination? What areas of this support need to be strengthened? (nos. 94; 243-244)

6. How are the charisms of the wives identified, enhanced, and utilized in ministry? How are they integrated into the collaborative parish/agency effort to serve? (no. 192)

7. Describe how diaconal formation and ministry offer opportunities for the marriage bond to be enriched by the Sacrament of Holy Orders, just as public ministry is enriched by married ordained ministers. (nos. 66-68; 139; 186; 246)

8. How are the restrictions on remarriage of the deacon after the death of his spouse explained? (no. 69; 75; 216) How does the program explore with candidates the permanency of the Order of Deacon? (no. 77; 99)

9. What provisions are made for the continued support and participation of the widows of deacons and for their material and emotional support? (no. 74)

10. How does the formation program explore with candidates the nature and extent of the obligation of a deacon's lifelong promise of obedience to the diocesan bishop and the implications of this promise for his ministry and marriage? (nos. 30; 41-43)

For the Family Life Perspective category please check the rating which best describes your overall assessment.

❐ A. Programs, plans, and activities are adequate or better than adequate in this category.
❐ B. Additional development and/or revision is needed in the following components of this category.
Indicate number(s) _____
❐ C. This category will require significant restructuring and/ or redesign.

Ministry and Life after Ordination

Ministry and Life of the Permanent Deacon
1. Describe how ministry assignments are made. Describe the ministry agreements or covenants and how responsibilities are delineated. What period of time do they cover? (no. 42; 44; 93)

2. Describe what structures are available to co-ordinate and provide mutual support to deacons and wives, and to nourish and maintain community among deacons, (e.g. through the deaneries, regional, or diocesan diaconal communities, placement, etc.) (nos. 47; 54; 260; 286-291).

3. Describe any diocesan policies regarding ecclesiastical garb and titles to be used by deacons. Describe how these policies enhance or restrict the deacon's relationship with others (nos. 88-89).

4. How does diaconal life and ministry in the diocese integrate the three general areas of diaconal ministry: Word, sacrament, and charity? (nos. 31-40; 79-84)

5. Describe the types of ministries deacons are involved in. Are these ministries consistent with the service/charity ministry of the deacon? (no. 48)

6. Describe how deacons are involved in collaborative ministry and are enablers of others in ministry (nos. 50; 55-56).

7. Is there a diocesan council or assembly of deacons? How are members chosen? Are wives represented? What are the responsibilities of this body? To whom are they accountable? (nos. 290-291)

8. How are deacons and wives involved in coordinating and planning for diocesan diaconate ministry and formation? (no. 281; 285; 289)

9. How are deacons considered and appointed to diocesan boards, committees and councils for planning and dialogue? (no. 49)

10. What policies exist concerning remuneration and benefits for deacons engaged in part-time and full-time ministry? (nos. 94-95)

11. Do deacons receive appropriate remuneration for the expenses incurred in the exercise of their ministry? (no. 96)

12. Describe how deacons are involved in the ministries of word and sacrament (nos. 79-83).

13. How does the diaconate community reflect the cultural reality and diversity of the local church? (nos. 161-164)

14. Describe what opportunities are provided for deacons to deepen and nurture their spirituality (nos. 62-64).

15. What provisions are there for integrating the ethnic, racial, cultural, and geographic communities with the mainstream of the diaconal community? (nos. 144-145)

16. How are deacons informed of their canonical responsibilities and obligations, as well as their canonical rights, by virtue of being incardinated in the diocese? Do deacons receive a written statement from the diocesan bishop identifying their canonical faculties? (nos. 42; 44-45)

17. Describe how deacons are made aware of the diocese's incardination and excardination policies (no. 78).

18. Do clear policies exist for a deacon who is moving to another diocese or for a deacon who is moving into the diocese? (no. 102)

For the Ministry and Life After Ordination category please check the rating which best describes your overall assessment.

❏ A. Programs, plans, and activities are adequate or better than adequate in this category.
❏ B. Additional development and/or revision is needed in the following components of this category.
       Indicate number(s) _____
❏ C. This category will require significant restructuring and/ or redesign.

Post-Ordination Path in Diaconal Formation

1. Describe the program for newly ordained (nos. 46; 250-252).

2. Describe the diocesan post-ordination program (nos. 42; 239-256).

3. What provisions are made for the continuing formation, spiritual growth, and supervision of deacons and wives? How is the deacon held accountable for continuing formation/education in each dimension: human, spiritual, intellectual, and pastoral? (nos. 251; 285-289)

4. What dimensions of continuing formation need to be strengthened? (nos. 241-249)

5. Is regular supervision provided for deacons? How and by whom? (no. 251)

6. What formation or training is provided for such supervisors? (nos. 251; 285-289)

For the Post-Ordination Path category please check the rating which best describes your overall assessment.

☐ A. Programs, plans, and activities are adequate or better than adequate in this category.
☐ B. Additional development and/or revision is needed in the following components of this category.
       Indicate number(s) _____
☐ C. This category will require significant restructuring and/ or redesign.

Relationships with Priests, Religious, and Laity

1. Describe the continuing catechesis on diaconal ministry, to assist the bishop, priests, religious, and laity to discern the needs and challenges of the local church (no. 43).

2. How is the diaconate presented and integrated with other ministries in the diocese? (nos. 48-49; 61)

3. What is the attitude of the local community, including laity, priests, and religious, toward the diaconate? (nos. 58 and 61)

4. What opportunities exist locally and within the diocese for deacons and priests to nurture a genuine respect for each other, while recognizing the integrity of their two distinct ministries? (no. 52)

5. How has the presbyterate received an appropriate catechesis about the diaconate? (no. 53)

6. How does the presbyterate support the ministry of deacons? (nos. 50-53)

7. How do deacons take an active role in promoting and inspiring the participation of the laity in the Church? (nos. 56-57)

8. Describe the relationship between deacons and women religious in the diocese. (no. 55)

For the Relationships with Priests, Religious, and Laity category please check the rating which best describes your overall assessment.

☐ A. Programs, plans, and activities are adequate or better than adequate in this category.
☐ B. Additional development and/or revision is needed in the following components of this category.
        Indicate number(s) _____
☐ C. This category will require significant restructuring and/ or redesign.